Understanding and Teaching

COHESION COMPREHENSION

Judith W. Irwin, Editor
Loyola University of Chicago

Published by the

INTERNATIONAL READING ASSOCIATION
800 Barksdale Road, Box 8139
Newark, Delaware 19714

INTERNATIONAL READING ASSOCIATION

Copyright 1986 by the
International Reading Association, Inc.

Library of Congress Cataloging in Publication Data
Main entry under title:

Understanding and teaching cohesion comprehension.

 Includes bibliographies.
 I. Reading comprehension – Addresses, essays, letures. 2. English language – Study and teaching – Addresses, essays, lectures. I. Irwin, Judith Westphal. II. International Reading Association.
 LB1050.45.U52 1986   428.4'3   85-14340
 ISBN 0-87207-964-3

Contents

PART ONE   What Is Cohesion Comprehension?

PART TWO   Research on Cohesion Comprehension

Contributors

John G. Barnitz
University of New Orleans
New Orleans, Louisiana

James F. Baumann
Purdue University
West Lafayette, Indiana

Charles H. Clark
Western Illinois University
Macomb, Illinois

Anne E. Gottsdanker-Willekens
Antelope Valley College
Lancaster, California

Judith W. Irwin
Loyola University of Chicago
Chicago, Illinois

Alden J. Moe
Louisiana State University
Baton Rouge, Louisiana

Cynthia J. Pulver
Purdue University-North Central Campus
Westville, Indiana

Jennifer A. Stevenson
International Reading Association
Newark, Delaware

Foreword

Having devoted much of my academic energy during my graduate school and early professorial days to the issue of cohesion and its effect on comprehension (unfortunately, we did not call it cohesion because we did not have the benefit of Halliday and Hasan's seminal treatment of the topic), I am honored to be able to introduce this book to the membership of the International Reading Association.

The intent of the volume, so ably organized and edited by Judith Irwin, is to improve student comprehension of the texts we hold them accountable for in our schools, by raising the level of awareness and understanding of teachers, administrators, teacher educators, and researchers about this important topic. There are three levels at which the contributors to this volume attempt to accomplish their goal, each corresponding to one of the three main parts of the book. At the first level, Irwin and her colleagues hope to provide us with an answer to the question, "Just what is cohesion anyway?" At the second level, they help us answer the question, "What do we know about cohesion and its effect on comprehension?" And at the third level (and in Part 3 of the book), they provide us with their beginning of an answer to the question, "In your own classroom or school, what can you do instructionally to promote better comprehension through activities that focus on cohesion?" It is my impression, after reading the volume, that it is best read in order to seek answers to all three questions, but that it can be read to seek an answer to any one of the questions. Teachers and administrators will find a wealth of useful and enjoyable instructional strategies and activities, particularly in Part 3.

In terms of the entire publication effort of the International Reading Association, this volume represents another example of what is becoming one of our most popular genres of books—an explicit attempt, in a single volume, to integrate issues of *theory, research,* and *practice.* These volumes are important to the organization and to the field because they represent the best of what can occur when we all work together on issues that lie at the heart of literacy. We congratulate Judith Irwin and her colleagues for contributing to this effort.

P. David Pearson
University of Illinois

Introduction

This is a book about teaching students to understand how sentences tie together. My commitment to the importance of this skill began when a teacher told me the story of a student who could not do a simple context clue exercise. When the teacher finally gave up and showed her the answers, the student was amazed: "I didn't know you could get answers from different sentences!" she exclaimed. This student thought of prose as groups of unconnected sentences to be comprehended one-by-one.

This is, of course, not the case. Authors and readers use many devices to link sentences together. Conjunctions, repetitions, and pronouns are examples. Together, these devices make up the "cohesion" of a passage. Teaching students to understand these devices can be called "teaching cohesion comprehension." Hence, our title.

Of course, we are not implying that all students need to be taught all aspects of cohesion comprehension. This is clearly not the case. Many students learn to comprehend these devices on their own, as is true of many comprehension skills.

Thus, this book represents an attempt to help teachers and reading specialists at all levels to a better understanding of the concept of cohesion and its relationship to comprehension. It also offers a large number of creative teaching suggestions from which the skillful teacher can pick and choose when appropriate. Part One includes chapters designed to explain the concept of cohesion and to help the reader informally analyze cohesion in written materials. A chapter dealing specifically with understanding types of anaphora is also included. Part Two includes extensive research reviews for those who would like to think more deeply about these concepts. It ends with the description of a study on cohesion in actual textbooks for children. Finally, Part Three, the longest and most important section, contains methods for teaching various kinds of cohesion comprehension. The authors have attempted to give teachers a variety of choices and to provide activities that are adaptable to all grade levels and to both classroom and remedial situations.

Of course, this is just a start. Future research will undoubtedly contribute new and exciting methodology for helping students tie sentences together. We hope that our readers will use this book as a catalyst for further research and teaching in this area.

JWI

Part 1
What Is Cohesion Comprehension?

Alden J. Moe
Judith W. Irwin

1

Cohesion, Coherence, and Comprehension

One important finding of recent research is that text cohesion is related to comprehension. (See Chapter 4 herein.) We contend that cohesion relations that bind individual sentences together help the reader to establish a coherent memory representation. Because of this, a clear understanding of cohesion can help educators predict comprehension problems, write comprehensible materials, and teach cohesion comprehension processes. Thus, this chapter describes the concept of cohesion, the distinction between cohesion and coherence, and the relationship of cohesion and coherence to comprehension. An example of an informal cohesion analysis is also presented.

Cohesion

The most definitive treatments of cohesion are provided by Gutwinski (2) and Halliday and Hasan (3). They agree that cohesion is achieved through relationships in which the interpretation of one idea in the text depends on successful interpretation of another. Cohesion may also be viewed as a type of redundancy which links one sentence or phrase with another. It is important to note that the term "cohesion in text" was intro-

Adapted from Alden J. Moe, "Cohesion, Coherence, and the Comprehension of Text," *Journal of Reading,* 1979, *23,* 16-20; and Judith W. Irwin, "Cohesion and Comprehension," *Illinois Reading Council Journal,* 1982, *10,* 5-8.

duced by Halliday "explicitly for the purpose of linguistic analysis" (2) and, as such, should be thought of as something that exists within text but not necessarily within a reader's mind. It is also important to emphasize that "cohesion" is not another name for discourse structure. Rather, cohesion is used to "show how sentences, which are structurally independent of one another, may be linked together" (3).

The links that establish cohesion are called *ties,* and a single instance of cohesion is a *cohesive tie.* Cohesion may be intra- or intersentential; both types are found in the following sentences:

David is going to buy his wife a new car.
She wants a new Buick for her birthday.

An intrasentence cohesive tie is found in the first sentence, connecting "David" and "his." Intersentence ties exist between "she" and "wife," "new" and "new," "Buick" and "car," and "her" and "wife." All of these ties are anaphoric (related back), as most cohesive ties are, although cataphoric (related forward) ties also provide cohesion in text.

Although relatively uncommon in school textbooks, cataphoric ties are occasionally found in the introductory sentences of short stories where the meaning of "it" is not clear for several sentences — and in some cases several paragraphs. Note the use of "it" in the following passage:

> It had happened before and it would probably happen again. It wasn't Jane's fault. It was Michael's; he simply hadn't expected so many guests and he didn't know that they would be so hungry.

While the meaning of "it" may not be completely clear, it becomes more apparent as more of the text appears. Ostensibly, the meaning of "it" may become quite clear with the addition of the following sentences.

> As in previous years, Jane and Michael held a party for the new faculty members. Jane had sent invitations to thirty-one guests, but Michael had expected only twenty.

Halliday and Hasan (3) have identified five distinct types of cohesion: reference, substitution, ellipsis, conjunction, and lexical cohesion. Each of the five categories is represented by particular features such as repetitions, omissions, uses of certain words, or the occurrences of certain constructions. Halliday and Hasan also provide a rather elaborate coding scheme for analyzing text in terms of number and types of cohesive ties. Their system allows for the quantification of the total number of cohesive ties and the identification of types of cohesive ties in a text.

A possible shortcoming of the system exists, however, in the fact that in the quantification of ties it is not possible to determine the strength of the tie that links the semantic relationships. Such a determination is related more to psychological analysis, and the Halliday and Hasan system is intended to be used only for linguistic analysis.

Examples of Types of Cohesive Ties

Type	Example
Reference (includes many types of pronouns)	*John* went to the store. *He* bought an apple.
Substitution (the replacement of one word or phrase within another)	Joan already *knows*. Everyone *does*. ("does" substitutes for "knows")
Ellipsis (the omission of a repeated word or phrase)	Would you like an *apple*? I have twelve. (implied repetition of apple)
Conjunction (includes additive, adversative, causal, and temporal links)	John went to the store *before* the rain began.
Lexical – Reiteration	An apple is a *fruit*. All *fruits* contain seeds.
Lexical – Collocation (co-occurrences of words which regularly co-occur in the language)	The apple cost fifty *cents*. I had a *dollar.*

Cohesion and Coherence

Cohesion is only one component of coherence. In addition to cohesion, at least one other factor must be present for a text to have coherence; that factor is organization (*15*). Other factors like situational consistency add coherence to text. Linguists consider cohesion to be a measurable linguistic phenomenon, whereas coherence is considered to be more global and is not as directly amenable to evaluation.

This is similar to the distinction that can be made between "local" and "global" coherence (*5*). While "global coherence" refers to the relationship between each sentence and the general topic of the whole passage, "local coherence" refers to the relationships between specific adjoining sentences. Thus, operationally, "cohesion" usually refers to the same thing as "local coherence" or "local connectedness" (*11*).

Cohesion exists within text and adds to the coherence of text. It may be useful to think of *coherence* as something the reader establishes—or hopes to establish—in the process of reading connected discourse; in this respect, coherence may be viewed as the cognitive correlate of cohesion. Generally, however, cohesion is a text related phenomenon, coherence is both a text related and a reader related phenomenon, and they are not synonymous.

Cohesion, Coherence, and Comprehension

For readers who must establish a coherent memory structure, cohesive ties can be very helpful. "It is the continuity provided by cohesion that enables the reader...to supply all the missing pieces, all the components of the picture which are not present in the text but are necessary to its interpretation" (3). If a text displays cohesion, that is, if the reader can find measurable semantic relationships in the text, it follows that the reader will establish coherence more easily than if little or no cohesion exists; recent research (4,10) suggests that this is indeed the case. In these studies, less cohesive text resulted in less efficient comprehension.

For the fluent reader, comprehension is usually an automatic process and makes low demands on the reader's cognitive resources (7,9). When unable to establish coherence from the text, the reader will stop normal cognitive processes to search long term memory or to make linking inferences. Research indicates that the more linking inferences the text requires, the heavier the reader's processing load (7,8).

In addition, the ability to infer implicit cohesion relations may be related to reading ability and prior knowledge. Paris and Upton (12) found that students develop the ability to infer intersentential relationships as they mature. Bridge, Tierney, and Cera (1) found that high ability third grade readers were more likely to make necessary causal and conditional inferences than were low ability third graders. Pearson, Hansen, and Gordon (14) found that for second graders prior knowledge was significantly related to the comprehension of inferable information.

Predicting Comprehension Problems

Thus, teachers should find it useful to be able to predict the places where comprehension might break down because of unclear cohesive relationships, particularly when giving reading assignments to younger or low ability readers.

The most serious coherence breaks seem to occur between main clauses. The teacher interested in assessing the cohesion of an assignment might, therefore, examine the relationships between each pair of adjoining clauses. This process is simple and quick and, though not scientifically rigorous, should be reasonably accurate in predicting where coherent interpretations might falter.

Consider the following extreme examples:

Cohesive Version
1) In the 1800s, Hawaii was an independent republic. 2) The Hawaiians had settled there from all over the world, 3) but most of them spoke English. 4) Because of this, Hawaiians wanted to become part of the United States. 5) In 1900, Hawaii was made a U.S. territory. 6) This resulted in increased trade with the United States, 7) and this brought great prosperity.

Noncohesive Version
1) In the 1800s Hawaii was an independent republic. 2) English was the dominant language. 3) In 1900, Hawaii was officially made a territory. 4) Increased trade with America brought prosperity.

The first thing to notice in comparing these versions is the difference in sentence and text length. The noncohesive version has shorter sentences and is less than half as long as the cohesive version. Indeed, in the process of shortening sentences and paragraphs, explicit links between sentences are sometimes lost (13), and texts with a carefully controlled readability level may be difficult to comprehend because of a lack of cohesion.

An examination of the cohesive version reveals no cohesion breaks. Sentence two is linked to sentence one by the repetition of the concept of Hawaii in both the reference to Hawaiians and the word "there." The third main clause is linked to the second main clause by the pronoun "them," and the fourth main clause is linked to the third main clause by means of an explicitly stated causal relationship. The references to the United States and the conceptual similarity of "become part of" and "territory" link main clauses four and five, and main clauses five and six are connected by an explicit causal relationship. Finally, the seventh main clause is linked to the sixth main clause by means of the demonstrative "this," which refers to the event in the previous clause.

In contrast, serious cohesive breaks are present in the noncohesive version; many inferences are required for a coherent interpretation. The reader must link sentence two to sentence one by inferring that English was the dominant language *in Hawaii in the 1800s.* The causal relationship between the language factor and the event of becoming a territory must be inferred to link sentences two and three. This requires a fairly sophisticated prior knowledge of the role of language in cultural and political identification. Finally, the causal relationship between the last two sentences must also be inferred.

A careful examination of the cohesion in reading assignments is fairly simple and may sometimes result in unexpected conclusions. In this case, the passage with the lower readability level clearly presents some critical comprehension problems not present in the other passage. A teacher who is aware of these problems will be much more likely to be able to help students with comprehension problems than one who is not aware of them.

Another implication for teachers is that students who cannot understand cohesive relations are less likely to be successful comprehenders. The aspects of cohesion which are most likely to cause comprehension problems are pronominal anaphora and explicit and implicit connectives. (See Part 2 for reviews of the research in these areas.) Teachers should be alert to students who have problems understanding these relations so that they can teach them these skills. (Methods for teaching these skills are presented in Part 3.)

Summary

In order to foster reading development, educators must be aware of the factors within a text that affect understanding. The existing evidence suggests that cohesion helps the reader achieve coherence and therefore facilitates comprehension. Teachers can predict comprehension problems and facilitate successful comprehension with a quick, informal analysis of the cohesion in reading assignments. In addition, they can teach students about cohesion and coherence factors in their textbooks.

References

1. Bridge, C., R. Tierney, and M. Cera. "Inferential Operations of Children Involved in Discourse Processing," paper presented at the National Reading Conference annual meeting, New Orleans, December 1977.
2. Gutwinski, W. *Cohesion in Literary Texts.* The Hague: Mouton, 1976.
3. Halliday, M.A.K., and R. Hasan. *Cohesion in English.* London: Longman, 1976.
4. Irwin, J.W. "The Effects of Linguistic Cohesion on Prose Comprehension," *Journal of Reading Behavior,* 1980, *12,* 325-332.
5. Irwin, J.W. "A Review of Procedures for Analyzing Coherence in Written Language Samples," *Diagnostique,* 1982, *8,* 43-51.
6. Irwin, J.W. *Teaching Reading Comprehension Processes.* Englewood Cliffs, NJ: Prentice-Hall, 1986.
7. Kintsch, W., and T.A. van Dijk. "Toward a Model of Text Comprehension and Production," *Psychological Review,* 1978, *85,* 363-394.
8. Kintsch, W., and D. Vipond. "Reading Comprehension and Readability in Educational Practice and Psychological Theory," in L.G. Nilsson (Ed.), *Memory: Process and Problems.* Hillsdale, NJ: Erlbaum, 1978.
9. LaBerge, D., and S.J. Samuels. "Toward a Theory of Automatic Information Processing in Reading," *Cognitive Psychology,* 1974, *6,* 293-323.
10. Marshall, N., and M.D. Glock. "Comprehension of Connected Discourse. A Study into the Relationships between the Structure of Text and Information Recalled," *Reading Research Quarterly,* 1978-1979, *14,* 10-56.
11. McCutchen, D., and C.A. Perfetti. "Coherence and Connectedness in the Development of Discourse Production," *Text,* 1982, *2,* 113-139.
12. Paris, S., and L. Upton. "Children's Memory for Inferential Relationships in Prose," *Child Development,* 1976, *47,* 660-668.
13. Pearson, P.D., and D.D. Johnson. *Teaching Reading Comprehension.* New York: Holt, Rinehart and Winston, 1978.
14. Pearson, P.D., J. Hansen, and C. Gordon. *The Effects of Background Knowledge on Young Children's Comprehension of Explicit and Implicit Information.* Urbana: Center for the Study of Reading, University of Illinois, Technical Report No. 116. (ED 169 521)
15. Perfetti, C.A., and A.M. Lesgold. "Discourse Comprehension and Sources of Individual Differences," in M.A. Just and P.A. Carpenter (Eds.), *Cognitive Processes in Comprehension.* Hillsdale, NJ: Erlbaum, 1977.

James F. Baumann
Jennifer A. Stevenson

2

Identifying Types of Anaphoric Relationships

Chapter 1 describes the concept of textual cohesion. This chapter defines and classifies one particular type of textual cohesion: anaphoric relationships. We begin first with a definition of anaphora. Second, we briefly review listings or taxonomies of anaphoric relationships developed by other writers. Third, we present a Selective Taxonomy of Anaphoric Relationships, a unique taxonomy which we developed for use in instruction, rather than for linguistic or research uses. We conclude the chapter with a discussion of recommended uses of the Selective Taxonomy.

Definition of Anaphora

With the growing interest in the relationships between cohesive ties in text and reading comprehension, several definitions of the specific cohesive element of anaphora have been offered. (Note that *anaphora* is the plural form of the singular *anaphor*.) A number of writers have provided operational definitions of anaphora in order to focus research on readers' abilities to resolve anaphoric relationships in written texts, to hypothesize about cognitive processes, or to analyze linguistic situations that contribute to anaphora resolution (*1,7,14*).

The most comprehensive (and elaborate) definition of anaphora can be found in Halliday and Hasan's *Cohesion In English* (*4*) in which anaphora are defined in relation to these authors' taxonomy of cohesive ties in text. A very simple and straightforward definition of anaphora is that noted by Pearson and Johnson (8). Their definition, taken from *The Random House Dictionary of the English Language* (13), defines anaphora as "the use of a word as a regular grammatical substitute for a preceding word or group of words." For example, in sentence (1), *she* is substituted for *Mary,* and *it* is substituted for *door.*

(1) Mary closed the door and then she locked it.

In example (2), the word *so* is substituted for several words (Gary is late).

(2) Gary might be late. If so, we'll start without him.

Building on the definitions presented by all these previous writers, we will use, within this chapter, the following definition.

> *Anaphora* are linguistic devices which signal the coreferential identity, or near identity, of two concepts; language relationships in which a word or phrase is used in place of another word or phrase which has been introduced previously.

Our definition of anaphora contains three important elements:

   A. the referent or antecedent (i.e., the first coreferential concept, that which is later referred to by the second coreferent);
   B. the reference item, which we will call the anaphoric term (i.e., the second coreferential item, which refers back to the first idea already mentioned);
   C. the relationship between A and B.

For example, in (3), the antecedent (Part A) is *cellar*, the anaphoric term (Part B) is *there,* and the relationship between A and B (Part C) is that *there* refers to, or takes the place of, *cellar.*

(3) Don't go down to the cellar. It's too cold there.

We emphasize the third part of our definition, the relationship between the anaphoric term and the antecedent, in spite of its obvious nature, because it is a reader's recognition of the coreferential identity or near identity of the first two parts of anaphora (A and B) that is critical for resolution or comprehension of anaphoric relationships. Since these relationships are usually implicit rather than explicit in text, readers must infer these coreferential links for complete comprehension.

It should be noted that we discuss only anaphoric relationships in this chapter, although other coreferential relationships also exist in text. Cataphora, for example, are other types of coreferential relationships. *Cataphora,* like anaphora, involve a cohesive tie between two concepts but, in cataphoric relationships, the reference term *precedes* the referent or antecedent. (Or, as Tierney and Mosenthal (11) state, cataphora involve "presupposing an item that appears in subsequent text" (p. 71).) For example, in (4) the cataphoric term *they* is introduced before the referent *whole crowd* appears in the text.

Baumann and Stevenson

(4) They waited in silence for a moment, and then the whole crowd broke into a wild cheer.

Cataphora are far less common in text than are anaphora.

A second form of coreference that will be noted but not discussed further in this chapter is *exophora*. In exophora, the referents are *outside the text*, not within the text. For example, in (6) the pronoun *it* in the last sentence refers exophorically to *snowman*, which is not available in the text and must be inferred from prior knowledge (9).

(6) The children were outside all morning trying to make one that looked just right. They had so much fun that the snow didn't even feel cold. Susie stuck on a carrot nose and coal eyes, and John found a hat and a pipe. They both thought it was the best one they had ever made.

In essence, exophoric relationships are based on what Pearson and Johnson (8) refer to as scriptally implicit information – information which must come from prior knowledge (reader's scripts) outside the text. In exophoric anaphora, the antecedent (Part A) is scriptally implicit.

Existing Taxonomies of Anaphoric Relationships

Several researchers and linguists have attempted to classify anaphoric relationships in text (*1,2,3,5,6,12*), usually for the purpose of anaphora resolution research. Two other comprehensive and useful listings of anaphora, the two taxonomies upon which our taxonomy is based, have been prepared by Halliday and Hasan (*4*) and Pearson and Johnson (*8*), and we will describe these taxonomies briefly.

Halliday and Hasan

As was described in Chapter 1, Halliday and Hasan have presented a detailed and complex model of cohesion in text. Although our discussion of Halliday and Hasan is somewhat redundant with information presented in Chapter 1, we have included it here since we present our Selective Taxonomy of Anaphoric Relationships by contrasting it to existing taxonomies. Since we have drawn so heavily from work by Halliday and Hasan in developing our taxonomy, it is critical that the reader understand how the Selective Taxonomy is similar to and different from these previous authors' work.

Halliday and Hasan describe five major types of cohesive ties: reference, substitution, ellipsis, lexical, and conjunction.

1. *Reference* occurs when the antecedent and the anaphoric term corefer to exactly the same idea, although their grammatical functions may differ. Reference includes simple personal pronouns (e.g., *he, she, they*), demonstrative pronouns (e.g., *this, these, that*), and comparatives (e.g., in

" 'You gave Tom three marbles. Why didn't you give me the same?' asked Kathy," *same* refers to, or compares to, three marbles).

2. *Substitution* occurs when one linguistic item replaces another and also adds some information which contrasts with the original antecedent idea. For example, in "My bicycle is old. I need a new one," *one* substitutes for *bicycle*, and *new* contrasts with *old*. Substitution can occur on the nominal (word), verbal, and clausal level.

3. *Ellipsis* occurs when a linguistic term is simply omitted, or, as Halliday and Hasan say, there is "substitution by zero." For example, in " 'How many books do you want?' asked Randy. 'Two,' answered Ralph," it is understood that Ralph actually substituted, but omitted, "two *books.*" Like substitution, ellipses can occur on the nominal (word) level, as in the above example, or on the verbal or clausal levels.

4. *Lexical* cohesion occurs when the same term, a synonymous term, or a superordinate linguistic term is used in place of a preceding term. In lexical cohesion, the two coreferents have the same meaning and the same grammatical function. For example, in "The deer wandered into the clearing. The animal was looking for a drink," the superordinate term *animal* is used in place of *deer.*

5. *Conjunction* occurs when semantic connections are made between two ideas, so that one's understanding of the second idea relates to one's understanding of the first idea. For example, in "He doesn't finish work until 10:30, so the party won't begin until 11:00," *so* is the conjunctive cohesive element linking the two sentences.

It should be noted that, although the first four types of cohesive ties described by Halliday and Hasan may be anaphoric according to our definition of anaphora, the fifth type is not. That is, the conjunctive *so* in the preceding example denotes a connection between the ideas contained in the two clauses of the example sentence, and therefore it is a cohesive tie. However, *so* does not denote a coreferential anaphoric situation in which a subsequent word or phrase replaces a preceding word or phrase. Another point to note about Halliday and Hasan's taxonomy is that it is intended to be linguistically descriptive, not educationally applicable; that is, the goal of these authors was to describe cohesion in English, not to prescribe what or how cohesive elements should be taught. Finally, note that the classification of cohesion within these authors' taxonomy is based primarily upon a description of anaphoric terms rather than antecedents—Part B rather than Part A of our definition of anaphora. In other words, each of the five types of cohesive ties is defined in terms of the reference item not in terms of the referent.

Pearson and Johnson

Pearson and Johnson (8) have prepared an eight part taxonomy of anaphoric relations. The Pearson and Johnson taxonomy is similar to Halliday and Hasan's in that the classification system is based upon the reference item. It differs from the Halliday and Hasan listing in that it is educationally based and is more readily translated into instructional practices and materials. That is, Pearson and Johnson propose that their classification system be used more for teaching purposes than as a comprehensive linguistic description. The eight entries in the Pearson and Johnson anaphora taxonomy include pronouns, locative pronouns, deleted nouns, arithmetic anaphora, class inclusive anaphora, inclusive anaphora, deleted predicate adjectives, and proverbs.

1. *Pronouns* include simple personal pronouns (e.g., *he, we, her, them*).

2. *Locative pronouns* consist of *here* and *there* (e.g., The class walked to the park, and Tommy left his baseball glove there).

3. *Deleted nouns* are usually replaced by adjectives. For example, in "The members of the soccer team were supposed to be at the field by 9:00 a.m., but only a few were there on time," the adjective *few* replaces the deleted noun *team members.*

4. *Arithmetic anaphora* are similar to deleted nouns but denote number. For example, in "Todd and Lisa walked down the hall. The former is tall and wide and the latter is short and skinny," *former* refers to *Todd,* and *latter* refers to *Lisa.*

5. *Class inclusive anaphora* are similar to Halliday and Hasan's lexical cohesion. For example, in "The leopard stalked the antelope, and the big cat ultimately pounced on its prey," *big cat* is a class inclusive term for *leopard.*

6. *Inclusive anaphora* are extensions of simple class inclusive anaphora in which an anaphoric term can refer back to an entire phrase, clause, or passage. For example, if a 500 word discussion of the immediate causes of World War I were followed by the concluding statement, "For these reasons, the United States entered World War I," then *for these reasons* would be an inclusive statement that refers to a major portion of the preceding text.

7. *Deleted predicate adjective* occurs when words such as *so is, is not, is too* indicate a deleted complement, as in "Mary is ambitious. Martha *is not,*" in which *ambitious* is deleted after *is not.*

8. *Proverbs* are analogous to pronouns in that the verb is substituted by a generic term such as *can, will* or *have.* For example, in "Rudolph got a perfect score on his spelling test, and so will Minnie," *so will* substitutes for *got a perfect score.*

A Selective Taxonomy of Anaphoric Relationships

Based on the work of Halliday and Hasan (*4*) and Pearson and Johnson (*8*), we have developed a Selective Taxonomy of Anaphoric Relationships, which is presented in the Table. The taxonomy is designed to be used for instructional purposes and is meant to be simple yet fairly comprehensive.

We adapted the Selective Taxonomy from an earlier version (*10*); in both versions we drew heavily from the ideas of the writers noted above.

Before describing specific aspects of the Selective Taxonomy, we should note several important general features. First, a feature that distinguishes the Selective Taxonomy from other listings of anaphora is that the major entries in the taxonomy are organized according to types of antecedents, rather than types of anaphoric terms. In other words, the three main entries—Noun Substitutes, Verb Substitutes, and Clausal Substitutes—describe *types of referents* for anaphora, rather than the specific anaphor itself. (However, subcategories within the three main sections do describe specific anaphoric terms, such as pronouns or synonyms.) We have adopted this organization because we believe it is simpler, more straightforward, and more useful for designing anaphora comprehension lessons and instructional materials, when compared to the more traditional anaphoric term organization, such as that used by Halliday and Hasan and Pearson and Johnson.

Second, the taxonomy is selective. That is, many varieties of anaphora, but certainly not all, are included. The taxonomy is selective so that it may be more useful educationally. We have included only those categories which seem to be critical for reading comprehension for school-age children, and only those anaphora types that are amenable to instruction. The Selective Taxonomy, therefore, contains only broad categories of anaphora presented in simple terms, so that teachers can easily understand the relationships and hence implement classroom instruction in these anaphora forms.

Finally, we have attempted to organize the Selective Taxonomy hierarchically. The three major categories in the taxonomy are Noun Substitutes, Verb Substitutes, and Clausal Substitutes, and they are arranged in that order since it seems reasonable, if not empirically validated, that situations in which the antecedent is a noun are easier to resolve than situations in which the antecedent is a verb or clause.

A closer look at the Selective Taxonomy, as shown in the Table, reveals the following characteristics. Within the first major portion of the Taxonomy, Noun Substitutes, are eight subtypes of anaphora. Several of these subcategories are taken directly from Halliday and Hasan or Pearson and Johnson or both (Personal Pronouns, Demonstrative Pronouns, Locative, Arithmetic); therefore, these require no further explanations. Anaphora Type I-A-3 (Noun Substitutes: Pronouns: Other) includes relative, interrogative, indefinite, reciprocal, reflexive, and intensive pronouns, and this category is not found in other taxonomies. All these pronouns are grouped together because they function in a similar manner and occur less frequently than the other pronoun entries. Anaphora Type I-C (Noun Substitutes: Temporal) is a new category, which includes noun substitutes that refer to time relations, such as *now, then,* and *before.* The next three categories, anaphora Types I-D (Synonym), Type I-E (Superordinate), and Type I-F (General Term) are adapted from categories described by Halliday and Hasan as instances of lexical cohesion. Synonym, Superordinate, and General Term are similar in that they relate pairs of nouns in text, but they differ in the specific relationships between the nouns. Synonym relationships occur when a synonymous term (*lad*) is substituted for a preceding term (*boy*). In Superordinate anaphoric relations, a superordinate anaphor (*animal*) is substituted for a preceding specific noun referent (*dog*). And in General Term relationships, a generic or general term (*problem*) is substituted for a preceding specific antecedent (*assaults*). The final category within Noun Substitutes anaphora, Type I-H (Deleted), is similar to Halliday and Hasan's ellipsis category on the nominal (word) level, in which an implied or unstated anaphoric term is "substituted" for a preceding antecedent. For example, in "Which blouse do you like? The green (   ) suits you well," a reader must mentally fill in *blouse* in the second sentence.

Anaphora Type II, Verb Substitutes, is a combination of the verbal parts of Halliday and Hasan's categories of substitution and ellipsis and of Pearson and Johnson's categories of deleted predicate adjectives and proverbs. There are three categories in Verb Substitutes: Inclusive, Deleted, and Deleted Predicate Adjectives. Inclusive verb substitutes occur when helping verbs or generic verb forms (e.g., *do, does, can, will*) substitute for preceding verb antecedents. For example, in "Tommie didn't eat his peas, but you did," *did* substitutes for *did eat*. Deleted verb anaphora are similar to deleted noun anaphora (Type I-H) in that the reader must mentally fill in part of a previously stated idea. For example, in "Alice sings well, but Harriet does not," a reader must infer that *sings well* is needed to complete the second clause of the sentence. Finally, the Deleted Predicate Adjective category is taken directly from Pearson and Johnson and consists of instances in which a reader must infer the presence of a previously stated verb complement. For example, in "José is athletic, but Juan is not," the reader must mentally complete the sentence by inserting *athletic* after *is not*.

Anaphora Type III, Clausal Substitutes, in the Selective Taxonomy consists of two subcategories: Inclusive and Deleted. These categories are analogous to the previously noted anaphora types of Inclusive and Deleted Verb Substitutes but, in these instances, entire clauses are substituted (Inclusive Clausal Substitutes) or deleted (Deleted Clausal Substitutes). These categories are similar to Halliday and Hasan's clausal forms of substitution and ellipsis.

To summarize, first, the Selective Taxonomy is organized according to three major types of antecedents (nouns, verbs, clauses). Second, it is selective, so that the few major categories and subcategories can be readily translated into instructional lessons and materials. Third, the Selective Taxonomy is arranged hierarchically, a hierarchy that is based more on common sense than on empirical data.

Selective Taxonomy of Anaphoric Relationships

Anaphora Type	Example of Anaphoric Term	Usage Example*
I. NOUN SUBSTITUTES		
A. Pronouns		
1. Personal		
a. Singular	I, my, mine, me, you, your, yours, she, her, hers, he, his, him, it, its	**John** and **Kitty** went to the store. *He* bought two gum drops, and *she* bought a candy bar. **Kitty** also bought a **candy apple,** but *she* was sad because *it* fell on the floor.
b. Plural	we, our, ours, us, you, your, yours, they, their, theirs, them	**Alice** and **Kathy** are best friends. *They* always play together. "Why don't *we* play with your kitten?" asked Alice. "All right," answered Kathy, "and let's invite Rosemary to play with *us*."
2. Demonstrative	this, that, these, those	"Look at all the **marbles** that have fallen on the floor," said Ralph. "Yes," replied Mike, "look at *these* green ones and *those* purple ones." "Yes," said Ralph, "but look at *this* whopper."
3. Other (relative interrogative, indefinite, reciprocal, reflexive, intensive)	who, that, which, each, what, whom, whose, whoever, some, any, none, somone, one, nobody, anyone, etc.	**Mark,** *who* just turned eleven, is the tallest boy in the class. The **problem of spitballs** is *one* that concerns me very much.
B. Locative	here, there	The family finally arrived at the **airport.** "*Here* we are," said Dad. "There's an **observation deck** upstairs. Let's go up *there*."
C. Temporal	now, then, before, after, later, earlier, sooner, etc.	"I'm supposed to stay in during **recess,** but I want to go out and play *then*." "How do you like it in **sixth grade**?" asked Jim. "Not very much," replied Max, "I liked fifth grade better." "Not me," said Jim, "I like it *now* much better."

D. Synonym	lad (antecedent: boy) cab (antecedent: taxi)	There's a **boy** in the tree. I hope the *lad* doesn't fall. The **taxi** sped down the street. The *cab* almost ran down a pedestrian because it moved so quickly.
E. Superordinate	animal (antecedent: dog) child (antecedent: boy) vehicle (antecedent: bus)	I heard a **dog** barking. The *animal* must have seen a cat. There's a **boy** in the tree. I hope the *child* will be careful. A **bus** went down the main street. The *vehicle* then turned down a side street.
F. General Term	problem (antecedent: assaults) thing (antecedent: treehouse)	**Assaults** have been on the increase. The police should take care of this *problem*. There is a boy up in the **treehouse**, and I'm afraid the old *thing* isn't very safe.
G. Arithmetic	one, some, all, none, few, many, several, couple, two, both, latter, former	**Mary** and **John** came in. The *former* is tall. The *latter* is short. The *two* make an interesting *couple*. *Both* are my friends.
H. Deleted		The **men** came home late. Both ( ) were tired. Have some **milk.** There isn't any ( ). Do all **monkeys** eat bananas? Most ( ) do. I like many **fruits**, but apples are the best ( ). Which **blouse** do you like? The green ( ) suits you well.

---

*The antecedents are shown in boldface type, and the anaphoric terms are in italics. Deleted anaphoric items are indicated by parentheses.

II. VERB SUBSTITUTES

A. Inclusive

do, does, do the same, do likewise, do so, do that, don't, so is, so has,

I don't **know** these people but you do.
Will you **call** the doctor? I already *have*.
Angela is **sailing** to Greece. *So is* Joanie.
Tim can **catch** a ball. *So can* Matt.

B. Deleted

Has he been **working** every day? I don't think he has (   ).
Amy **sings** well. Mark cannot (   ).
Mom **likes bologna.** Dad does not (   ).

C. Deleted Predicate Adjective

John is **lost.** Susan is not (   ).
The lion was **large.** The tiger was (   ), too.

III. CLAUSAL SUBSTITUTES

A. Inclusive

so, not

Will **Mary Sue come tomorrow?** I think *not*.
John **was very disappointed**, and he said *so*.

B. Deleted

Who was **going to plant some trees?** John was (   ).
Who **broke the window?** Harry (   ).

*The antecedents are shown in boldface type, and the anaphoric terms are in italics. Deleted anaphoric items are indicated by parentheses.

Applications of the Selective Taxonomy

As previously stated, we have prepared the Selective Taxonomy of Anaphoric Relationships as a teaching tool. Therefore, we envision its greatest application to be in the educational realm, for use by teachers, educational writers, and publishers.

Classroom teachers or reading specialists can use the taxonomy as a guide in preparing lessons and materials for anaphora instruction. In Chapter 9 we present a strategy for teaching anaphora, several model lessons, and many practice and reinforcement exercises for classsroom use. The Selective Taxonomy can serve as the content source for teachers who desire to prepare anaphora lessons. Moreover, as we note in Chapter 9, although current reading instruction materials give little attention to anaphora instruction, for those lessons that are present (e.g., some basal readers have lessons on comprehending simple pronoun referents), the Selective Taxonomy can be used to extend or expand the lesson. An example of how this may be accomplished is also presented in Chapter 9.

Educational publishers and authors can also use the Selective Taxonomy as a content guide, in this case for the development of commercial materials on anaphora comprehension. We certainly see the need for expanded anaphora instruction in comprehension strands of basal reader programs and for the development of supplemental skill programs or packets on anaphora. The Selective Taxonomy can be a source for the development of these much needed materials.

Reading researchers may also find the Selective Taxonomy useful. These materials can be used to design studies to assess what anaphora types children comprehend, what types children have difficulty with, and when children have mastered these cohesive elements. Studies in these areas could then be synthesized so that an empirically based taxonomy and scope and sequence could be established.

To summarize, within this chapter we have defined anaphora and presented a Selective Taxonomy of Anaphoric Relationships. Our purpose has been to provide a taxonomy useful for the preparation of instructional lessons and materials. We hope that teachers and educational publishers find this taxonomy helpful in the development of reading curriculum and instruction, and that it will serve as a stimulus for further research on how children learn to comprehend these pervasive cohesive elements in written text.

References

1. Bormuth, J.R., J. Carr, J. Manning, and P.D. Pearson. "Children's Comprehension of Between- and Within-Sentence Syntactic Structures," *Journal of Educational Psychology,* 1970, *61,* 349-357.
2. Clark, H.H. "Inferences in Comprehension," in D. LaBerge and S.J. Samuels (Eds.), *Basic Processes in Reading: Perception and Comprehension.* Hillsdale, NJ: Erlbaum, 1977.

3. Crothers, E.J. "Inference and Coherence," *Discourse Processes,* 1978, *1,* 51-71.
4. Halliday, M.A.K., and R. Hansen. *Cohesion in English.* London: Longman, 1976.
5. Lesgold, A.M. "Variability in Children's Comprehension of Syntactic Structures," *Journal of Educational Psychology,* 1974, *66,* 333-338.
6. Menzel, P. "Anaphora," in J.R. Bormuth, *On the Theory of Achievement Test Items.* Chicago: University of Chicago Press, 1970.
7. Nash-Webber, B.L. *Inference in an Approach to Discourse Anaphora,* Technical Report 77. Urban, IL: Center for the Study of Reading, 1978.
8. Pearson, P.D., and D.D. Johnson. *Teaching Reading Comprehension.* New York: Holt, Rinehart and Winston, 1978.
9. Stevenson, J.A. "Effects of Explicit-Activated and Implicit-Activated Antecedents on Average Third and Eighth Grade Readers' Resolution of Anaphora," unpublished doctoral dissertation, University of Wisconsin, Madison, 1980.
10. Stevenson, J.A., and J.F. Baumann. "Helping Children Comprehend Anaphoric Relationships (Pronouns, Pro-Verbs, Deleted Nouns): Definition, Research and Instructional Suggestions," paper presented at the International Reading Association annual convention, New Orleans, May 1981.
11. Tierney, R.J., and J. Mosenthal. "Discourse Comprehension and Production: Analyzing Text Structure and Cohesion," in J.A. Langer and M.T. Smith-Burke (Eds.), *Reader Meets Author/Bridging the Gap.* Newark, DE: International Reading Association, 1982.
12. Webber, B.L. *A Formal Approach to Discourse Anaphora.* New York: Garland Publishing, 1979.
13. Wolf, H.B. (Ed.). *Random House Dictionary of the English Language.* Springfield, MA: G. C. Merriam Company, 1966.
14. Yekovich, F.R., and C.H. Walker. "Identifying and Using Referents in Sentence Comprehension," *Journal of Verbal Learning and Verbal Behavior,* 1978, *17,* 265-277.

3   Charles H. Clark

Assessing Comprehensibility:
The PHAN System

Most teachers and professionals in reading are by now familiar with the shortcomings of traditional readability formulas. Such formulas do not account for concept load, organization, style, reader familiarity with the subject, or reader motivation and purpose. The fact that readability formulas based only on word and sentence length continue to be useful general indicators of text difficulty is as surprising to those who study the relationships between text and comprehension as it is reaffirming for those who rely upon their use (7).

Because of the heavy reliance of the formulas on vocabulary and sentence length, their primary focus is upon decodability rather than comprehensibility. Educators concerned with the comprehensibility of materials, whether they are considering them for adoption or evaluating the type and degree of preteaching needed to facilitate learning, must go beyond readability formulas to arrive at valid decisions. The purpose of this article is to describe a simple phrase analysis system called PHAN which can be used by anyone to assess the degree and nature of potential stumbling blocks to comprehension within a passage or book.

The basis for the phrase system lies with recent developments in the theoretical and empirical study of the comprehension process. Though at best a simplistic stepchild to the recently developed systems for analyzing prose (e.g., 6), a phrase system permits observation of some of the same aspects of prose, and at the same time is extraordinarily simple. The

Reprinted from *The Reading Teacher*, 1981, *34*, 670-675.

models of comprehension during reading and the analysis techniques developed by Kintsch and his colleagues (6,7) encourage reasonable hypotheses as to the relative difficulty a reader may encounter in a particular passage, the specific text areas that may present problems and the reason for those problems, and, with acknowledged nonconsideration of reader background and interest, the amount and type of information that is most likely to be retained. Such techniques are, however, time-consuming to learn and to use; the models themselves are complex and beyond the interest of most reading practitioners.

Using PHAN

The basic procedure in the phrase analysis or PHAN system is simply to divide the selection into phrases and list the individual phrases sequentially. There is no need for the phrase divisions to follow any particular rules as long as one is consistent within and between selections (for comparative reasons).

I have found certain guidelines helpful, however. Generally, small phrase divisions make analysis easier. Connectives such as *and* or *because*, verbal units, prepositional phrases, and nouns with their adjectives and determiners (e.g., *the*) constitute workable phrase boundaries. For example, in the sentence "Follow the yellow brick road and it will lead you to your goal," these divisions yield the following seven phrases: Follow/the yellow brick road/and/it/will lead/you/to your goal.

The following passage from the fifth level of the Ginn 360 Series (8) serves as an example.

Old Buildings and New

Men are working in the city.
They want to take down some old buildings.
The men work with big machines, and the old buildings come down.
Now the old buildings are down and new buildings are going up.
Men work with machines here, too.
Up go the new buildings.

Reference Cohesion

The separation into phrases as shown in the Example greatly facilitates examination of coherence factors. One of the easiest to analyze is reference cohesion, that is, the clarity of the relationships between pronouns and their referents (1,2). Phrases 1 and 4 in the Example illustrate this. The difficulty of perceiving the referent is measured by counting the number of phrases separating the pronoun from its referent. In this example, there should be no particular comprehension difficulty since the pronoun and its referent are separated by only two phrases. If the pronoun is too far from its referent or from a prior incidence of that pronoun, readers, and particularly poor readers, may have difficulty comprehending the pronoun because the referent may no longer be readily available in working memory. (Readers differ, but a separation of four or more phrases is sufficient to cause concern.) In the example passage, reference cohesion should not present a problem for the comprehender.

Connectives

The stilted language common in children's readers may cause comprehension difficulties through its use of connectives showing conjunction (*and, or*), causality (*because*), time (*after, then*), or location (*in, here*).

There are three ways in which misused connectives interfere with comprehension: They may be omitted, widely separated, or imprecise.

Phrase analysis example of "Old Buildings and New"

	Phrases	Number of phrase steps
	1. Men	⎤
	2. are working	⎥ 2
	3. in the city.	⎥
	4. They	⎦
	5. want	
Vocabulary problem	6. to take down	
	7. some	
	8. old buildings.	
	9. The men	
	10. work	⎤ ⎤
	11. with big machines	⎥
Inference	12. and	⎥ 3
	13. the old buildings	⎥
Vocabulary problem	14. come down.	⎦
Inference	15. Now	
	16. the old buildings	
	17. are down	
Inference	18. and	⎤ 2 14
	19. new buildings	⎥
Vocabulary problem	20. are going up.	⎦
	21. Men	
	22. work	
	23. with machines	
Inference	24. here	
Inference	25. too.	
Vocabulary problem	26. Up go	⎦
	27. the new buildings.	

Missing connectives. In the Example, there is one missing causal connective near phrase 25. The reader must realize that the men working with the machines are constructing the buildings. Spotting such missing connectives in children's literature is not always easy for adults because we make the necessary inference naturally. There are no serviceable guidelines for pinpointing the omissions; we simply must be aware of meaning units or phrases that are logically but not explicitly connected.

Two additional examples may be helpful: "John went to the store. Amy went to the store." "Tom washed the shirt. He put it on the line to dry." In the first, the reader is expected to realize that both John and Amy went to the store, and that these actions are connected. However, the connection is not explicit.

The second example is more subtle. These two sentences are logically related by sequence: First the shirt is washed, then it is dried. Though the logical relationship is evident to proficient adult readers, some beginners may be misled by the omission of an explicit connective such as *then.*

When the reader is forced to infer a missing connective, the inference process consumes processing capacity needed for other aspects of comprehension (7) thereby potentially decreasing comprehension and retention. In some cases this type of reference may even be beyond the reader's capabilities, which potentially affects overall comprehension due both to the missing element in the passage and the effort involved in attempts to understand related information. The omission of connectives in early reading materials is of course common because it allows shorter sentences, thus resulting in a lower readability formula score.

Separated connectives. By definition, connectives link sentence elements. When the elements are too far apart, comprehension is impeded, as it is with pronouns and referents.

The elements being connected must be available in current working memory. If one or both elements are no longer immediately accessible, the reader must reintroduce the information either by taking it from a less immediate memory or seeking it visually by regressing or making an inference. Any of these options can obviously disrupt comprehension (7).

In the Example, in phrase 25, the connective *too* probably links phrases 21-24 with phrases 9-11. (It is not entirely clear what is connected, which is another problem.) The easiest way to count the distance between connected elements is to count the number of phrases between the verb phrases involved. In the Example, the reader must either connect elements 14 phrases apart or construct an inference, either of which is difficult. The connectives in phrases 12 and 18 also require the linking of phrases separated by three and two elements respectively.

Imprecise connectives. Examples of incorrect use of connectives in the previous selection are phrases 12 and 18. The *and* in phrase 12 is a simple conjunctive connective, whereas a time connective showing sequence (or perhaps causality) is actually needed. It is important for the reader to realize that the buildings are destroyed as a result of and during the time when the men are working with the machines. As the sentence stands, a literal interpretation indicates that the working of the men and the destruction of the buildings are essentially unrelated. Similarly, phrase 18 should have a time reference indicating sequence, such as *after*. The reader must realize that the new buildings can be constructed only after the old buildings are destroyed. Both of these instances require that the reader make an inference.

Phrases 15 and 24 show imprecise connectives, which either result in vagueness or require inferences. The *now* in phrase 15 is apparently the writer's attempt to show the sequence of events, a problem discussed earlier. However, it is misplaced and has no temporal reference. A relative temporal reference such as *now* is difficult to understand unless we know what the time is. There is no earlier time reference on which to base phrase 15. Similarly, with phrase 24, the reader does not know where *here* is, and must infer that it refers to the place the machines were previously used (see phrase 10 and 11). This particular instance presents additional difficulties in that a complete understanding depends upon adequate comprehension of phrase 25, which has its own problems as discussed earlier.

Vocabulary

One final aspect of prose analysis where the phrase breakdown method is useful is in estimating vocabulary difficulty. Readability formulas do measure word difficulty with some efficiency. However, in connected prose a single word carries relatively little meaning; its meaning develops primarily through context. Accordingly, the phrase is a more realistic meaning element than is the isolated word and is a more appropriate basis for an evaluation concerned with comprehensibility. The passage from the Ginn series provides excellent examples of the importance of looking at phrases in context. In phrase 6, for instance, *take down* is two words with one meaning. The two words in isolation are considered readable at the targeted ability level (both are short and common), but as a meaning unit they may be beyond the students' grasp. There are similar problems in phrases 14, 20, and 26.

Using such multiword meaning units helps a publisher meet a predetermined readability formula level, but it may lead to "word calling" and have serious effects on comprehension. Whether a phrase presents vocabulary difficulty depends upon two factors—its context and the students' familiarity with the form. *Take down*, for instance, would be easily understood in terms of wash on a clothes line by most students for whom line drying is familiar but may present problems in reference to demolishing buildings. Conclusions can only be made with a knowledge of particular students.

Summarizing Results

Once the passage has been divided into phrases and coherence variables and vocabulary have been assessed, the results should be summarized. Three categories should be included: 1) the number of phrases between pronouns and referents, and between connected information; 2) the number of inferences needed; and 3) the number of potentially difficult phrase concepts, i.e., difficult multiword vocabulary. There will be a number for each category. In the Example, the results for the first two areas are variable, depending upon whether the reader can connect elements which are far apart or must construct an inference. The results for this passage are 21 phrase steps, 5 inferences, and 4 vocabulary phrases, as illustrated in the Example.

The totals in each of the three categories can be used to compare comprehensibility of passages having equal numbers of phrases. Passages with higher numbers may be expected to be harder to comprehend. Such materials should be avoided when possible at least for poor readers. When avoidance is impossible, the vocabulary, inference relationships, and pronouns can be discussed before reading. Preteaching of these specific areas should facilitate comprehension.

A final alternative is, of course, rewriting. With a phrase analysis like the above, particular areas which must be clarified are pinpointed and remedies are obvious (3). Rewriting, however, is time consuming and, as in the case of entire basals, often unreasonable, but it is well worth the effort to rewrite favorite stories, handouts, directions, instructions, and test materials.

Using PHAN with Conventional Measures

Though the PHAN system can be used for evaluating materials, pinpointing areas where preteaching may be valuable, and directing rewriting, it is not intended as an isolated technique. It does not yield an easily interpretable grade level score; it depends on comparisons with other similarly analyzed passages and on assessment of particular students' abilities.

When considering textbooks for adoption, it is usually helpful to begin assessment with conventional readability formulas which are objective and provide a grade level equivalency. The resultant readability level should then be evaluated by other methods of assessing reading difficulty, including the phrase analysis system of appraising comprehensibility and experimental use of the material with students. The cloze technique is often used to evaluate materials because it is relatively easy to administer, score, and interpret. Typical comprehension questions or story retelling after reading can also be used to assess the ability of students to deal with the material.

Frequently, the teacher can make an educated and directed evaluation of other aspects of the material affecting its readability. The teacher's evalu-

Clark

ation can then be compared with known student capabilities and interests. Irwin and Davis (5) recently developed a readability checklist that should make this type of evaluation more reliable by providing an explicit framework and guidelines.

Major adoption decisions should not be made without careful evaluation including the use of all the techniques mentioned. Readability is not a concept restricted to formulas or to decoding but must include evaluation of comprehensibility. Ultimately, readability depends not on the materials but on the abilities and interests of students.

References
1. Bean, T.W., T.C. Potter, and C.H. Clark. "Selected Semantic Features of ESL Materials and Their Effect on Bilingual Students' Comprehension," paper presented at the National Reading Conference Meeting, San Antonio, Texas, December 1979.
2. Chapman, J. "Confirming Children's Use of Cohesive Ties in Text: Pronouns," *The Reading Teacher*, 1979, *33*, 317-322.
3. Clark, C.H., and V.F. Stone. "Rewriting Material to Modify Readability: A Step Beyond Vocabulary and Sentence Length," paper presented at the Illinois Reading Council meeting, Peoria, March 1979.
4. Irwin, J.W. "Implicit Connections and Comprehension," *The Reading Teacher*, 1980, *33*, 527-529.
5. Irwin, J.W., and C. Davis. "Assessing Readability: The Checklist Approach," *Journal of Reading*, 1980, *24*, 124-130.
6. Kintsch, W., and T.A. van Dijk. "Toward a Model of Text Comprehension and Production," *Psychological Review*, 1978, *85*, 363-394.
7. Kintsch, W., and D. Vipond. "Reading Comprehension and Readability in Educational Practice and Psychological Theory," in L.G. Nilsson (Ed.), *Memory: Processes and Problems.* Hillsdale, NJ: Erlbaum, 1978.
8. "Old Buildings and New." *May I Come In?* Lexington, MA: Ginn, 1969.

Part 2
Research on Cohesion Comprehension

Judith W. Irwin

4

Cohesion and Comprehension:
A Research Review

Interest in relating text structure characteristics to comprehensibility is clearly not new, as evidenced by the seemingly unending number of readability formulas presently available (*42*). What is new is the ability to describe text structure at levels larger than the word or sentence. With an increasing number of linguists discussing text grammars (*22, 49, 52, 60* and others) and an increasing number of psychologists studying the comprehension of connected discourse (see *51*), it is not surprising that the structural characteristics described by the linguists are being tested for psychological reality.

One aspect of prose structure which is repeatedly discussed and investigated is cohesion. This chapter describes several approaches to the notion of cohesion and its role in comprehension in order to suggest directions for both psychological and educational research. If cohesion is related to comprehension, then developing a clear description of what it is and how it is related has important implications for teaching comprehension skills and for writing comprehensible textbooks.

It is important to distinguish "cohesion," as discussed in this review, from other text structure characteristics which contribute to the overall coherence of a passage. Cohesion can be loosely defined as the set of structures, both semantic and syntactic, which directly link sentences to each other. This is to be distinguished from things like topical unity, organizational patterns, story grammars, and macrostructures. The latter describe the relationship of each sentence to a larger or more abstract super-structure, thus describing how sentences are linked to each other by means of their relation to this higher level structure. In contrast, for the purposes of this review, cohesive relations are defined as those which link one sentence to another without reference to a higher level of analysis. Also for the purposes of this review, "coherence" will be defined as the combined effect of all the factors that contribute to textual unity, cohesion being one of them.

Describing Cohesion

Several linguists, in the process of developing text grammars, have included descriptions of various types of cohesive relations. The linguistic theories which have most directly influenced psychologists can be represented by those of Grimes (22), van Dijk (60) and Halliday and Hasan (26). Grimes discusses "cohesion" as "the way information in speech relates to information that is already available" (p. 272) and his thinking is largely based on the work of Halliday (24, 25). Basically, this theory states that information is linguistically blocked into units based on the amount of information that the speaker thinks is new to the hearer. This blocking may correspond to clausal boundaries or may be marked in some other way. Presumably, this blocking enables the hearer to focus on the new information in order to link it to what is already known, and this linking provides textual cohesion.

Van Dijk (60) presents a more global theory of "coherence" in which many aspects of language simultaneously contribute. Such things as connectives, implications, verb frames, property relations, condition-consequence relations, general-particular relations, and other semantic relations which link sentences are all said to add to the coherence of a text. Moreover, van Dijk points out that coherence relations are often implicit and that making every coherence relation explicit would result in a text that was "overcomplete" (p. 110) and unnatural. Finally, he also includes the notion of "topic" and "comment" in a system similar to the "old" and "new" information system described by Grimes.

Halliday and Hasan (26) systematically describe the specific semantic and syntactic relations which can link individual words in a text. "Cohesive ties" are defined as instances in which two words are linked by one of five types of relationships: 1) referential, including personal, demonstrative, and comparative pronouns; 2) substitution, the replacement of one word with another; 3) ellipsis, the omission of a repeated concept; 4) conjunction, including additive, adversative, causal, and temporal links; and 5) lexical, including reiterations of concepts and collocation. (See Chapter 1 in this book for examples.) At least one study (32) has found that the number of cohesive ties in a passage may be related to its readability, defined as reading time per 100 propositions recalled, and to prompted recall completeness in the delayed condition only. Other applications of cohesion analyses have also been suggested (47, 59).

Thus, several linguists (22, 26, 60) have presented descriptions of cohesion factors in language. However, as linguists, they do not describe the effects of these factors on cognitive processes. Psychological models are required to determine which of these linguistic descriptions has the most relevance for reading comprehension.

Relevant Psychological Theories

At least two recent psychological models of comprehension have included descriptions of cohesive relations which may have psychological reality (36, 40). Moreover, several models of inference processes also have implications concerning the role of cohesive relations during information processing. All of these psychological models selectively reflect the aforementioned linguistic theories.

For instance, the Kintsch and van Dijk (40) model of comprehension predicts that the first stage of processing input information involves selecting a set of propositions to be held in short term memory. (A "proposition" can be loosely defined as an "idea unit." Systems for analyzing the ideational structure of a passage in terms of propositions have been provided by Kintsch (38) and others.) When the next set of input propositions is processed, "coherence," is established by finding a shared semantic argument between the new set and the set retained in short term memory. If no shared referent is found, a reinstatement search of the long term memory of the previous text is required. It is hypothesized that the number of reinstatement searches required by a text provides a direct measure of "coherence." Kintsch (37) has reported that this measure correlated .62 with readability, defined as reading time per proposition recalled, and .59 with recall completeness.

Other data that support the relationship between such a measure and readability have been presented by Kintsch and Vipond (41). They found that the number of inferences required for coherence correctly predicted the direction of the differences among several passages in terms of reading times and numbers of saccades and fixations. Further support for this theory has also been found by Vipond (61) and Lesgold, Roth, and Curtis (45) who also found that the numbers of required reinstatement searches were related to comprehension efficiency.

Clearly, the presence of "coherence" in terms of shared arguments between retained and incoming information should also be related to cohesion as defined in this review. In fact, Irwin (31) did find that when the number of cohesive ties as defined by Halliday and Hasan (26) was varied so that one version of a passage had twice as many ties as the other, a subsequent proposition analysis indicated that the cohesive versions also had twice as many argument repetitions as did the less cohesive version.

Just and Carpenter (*36*) have suggested a model of comprehension based on eye movement data which similarly stresses the centrality of establishing coherence and the role of cohesive relations in contributing to this process. They postulate that interclause integration occurs continuously as the reader processes each word and clause, that is, whenever a "linking relation can be computed." They also hypothesize that there is a "sentence wrap-up" when the reader comes to the end of a sentence. During this stage, a reader finalizes interclause integration. Assigning referents and constructing connective relationships are examples of possible integrative processes.

Several recent theories concerning the role of inference in comprehension processes have similarly cited the establishment of coherence through the inference of cohesive and other relations as one of its fundamental purposes. Thorndyke (*58*) has described a model of inference in which the purpose of inference is "to provide an integrating context for the interpretation of incoming information in order to establish coherence and continuity in the text" (p. 437). Frederiksen (*19*) points out that relations between individual ideas are often implicit and, therefore, that children must develop "the ability to infer coherent interpretations." Hildyard and Olson (*29*) defined "enabling" inferences as "those which serve to provide a causal relationship between concepts or events" (p. 94) and found that intermediate grade children did not distinguish between these cohesive inferences and actual propositional content, whereas they did distinguish between pragmatic inferences which were "merely invited" and actual content.

In an extensive analysis of types of possible inferences, Crothers (*13,14*) suggests that inferences that are necessary for coherence should be considered part of the semantic text base. He states that in his taxonomy "the main purpose of many, though not all, of the proposed inference types is to explicate the implicit coherence of the passage" (*14*, p. 7). Such inferences include inferences of connective relationships, antecedents, consequents, coreference, synonymy, and antonymy, all of which contribute to the overall cohesion of the text.

At least one theory of inference which does not directly mention coherence or cohesion is also applicable. Clark (*9, 10*) describes a model of inference based on the Given-New Contract (*11, 27*) which is clearly related to the linguistic notion of old and new information. The hypothesis is that the reader/listener goes through three steps in comprehending: 1) identifying the given and new information, 2) searching memory for the antecedent to the old information, and 3) adding the new information to memory. Clark (*11*) describes a taxonomy of "implicatures" (p. 247) which are used to infer the referent of the given information marking, and this taxonomy contains categories of relations mentioned in descriptions of cohesion: 1) direct reference, including pronominalization and identity; 2) indirect reference by association; 3) indirect reference by characterization;

and 4) temporal relations, including reasons, causes, consequences, concurrences, and subsequences. Moreover, support for the facilitative effect of correct old and new information markings has also been found by Carpenter and Just (6).

Thus, several psychological models of comprehension and inference include descriptions of how and why cohesion is related to comprehension processes. Specifically, Just and Carpenter (36) and Kintsch and van Dijk (40) have presented models that show that establishing coherence between new and old information is critical for comprehension. Theories of inference describe how inferences are generated when readers are looking for implicit cohesion information.

Specific Cohesive Relations

Global models of the relationship between cohesive relations and various comprehension processes are difficult to investigate because of their complexity. Much research has examined the relationship between specific cohesive relations and processing difficulty. Though not always presented as studies concerned with cohesion, this research clearly provides important information regarding the nature of these effects.

Coreference

The most commonly discussed cohesive relation is coreference, that is, the situation in which one lexical unit refers to another. In the cohesion system of Halliday and Hasan (26), this would refer to reference, ellipsis, substitution, and, in some cases, lexical relations.

One type of coreference is the argument or word repetition included in the Kintsch and van Dijk (40) model, and this factor has been linked to comprehensibility in other studies. Kintsch and others (39) found that the number of word concepts in a passage was significantly related to reading time and recall completeness even though the numbers of words and propositions in the stimulus passages were controlled. Similarly, Entin and Klare (17) reported that, in a factor analysis of three correlation matrices of readability variables, a third factor found, after the traditional word and sentence level factors, was the number of different words used in the passage. Graesser, Hoffman, and Clark (21) found the number of new argument nouns to be a significant predictor of reading times.

Moreover, it seems that the facilitative effect of argument repetition may be affected by other factors. For instance, Yekovich and Walker (64) found that simple word repetition may not establish coherence unless coreference is established. In their study, coreference, as indicated by the definite article, resulted in shorter reading times than nonreferential repetition signaled by the indefinite article. Yekovich, Walker, and Blackman (63) similarly found that argument repetition lost its facilitative effect when the old/new markings were incorrect, and Yekovich and Manelis (*62*) found no facilitative effect for argument repetition in a delayed recall condition. Finally, Hayes-Roth and Thorndyke (*28*) found that integration was faster when the concept repetition used the same wording rather than a synonym.

The results of research comparing the comprehensibility effects of pronominal reference to the similar effects of argument repetition have been conflicting, and some evidence indicates that several aspects of pronoun reference may interact to determine its relationship to comprehension processes. Fishman (*18*) found no difference in the comprehensibility of pronouns and the comprehensibility of repeated words in term of a recognition task, whereas Lesgold (*43*) found that prompted recall for a sentence was greater when pronominal reference was used than when noun repetition was used. Clark and Sengul (*12*) found that reading times were shortest when the referent was in the preceding clause, but there was no difference between the referent being two sentences earlier or three sentences earlier. Finally, Barnitz (*3*) found that for children from grades two, four and six, forward reference was easier than backward reference, and noun phrase reference was easier than sentential reference. (For a more extensive review of the literature on anaphora, see Chapter 5.)

Semantic Relatedness

In the van Dijk (*60*) description, many semantic relations contribute to intersentential unity, and evidence does indicate the psychological reality of some of this description. In studies involving the monitoring of reading times on individual sentences, Carpenter and Just (*6*) found that it took less time to read a target sentence if that sentence contained a noun that was directly entailed by the verb in the preceding sentence. Thus, it could be hypothesized that a cohesive link is established by the semantic relation of entailment. These results were further supported by the results of a similar study (*56*) which used longer passages.

In addition, semantic relations other than direct entailment may also contribute to cohesion. Haberlandt and Bingham (*23*) manipulated the "relatedness" of verbs in the second sentence in sentence triples. For instance "Brian punched George" was followed by either "George called the doctor" or "George liked the doctor." In this case, relatedness depended on world knowledge about actions which are likely to take place in the context of other actions. They found that reading times were longer for the third sentence of the triples containing unrelated verbs than for the third sentence in the triples containing related verbs even though the third sentences were always identical.

Connective Concepts

In the Halliday and Hasan (*26*) and the van Dijk (*60*) descriptions, conjunction is said to contribute to the cohesion of a text, and there is some experimental evidence that the explicitness of connective concepts such as causality and conditionality may be related to recall completeness (34), at least for some readers. Marshall and Glock (46) found that subjects from a community college reading a passage in which conditional relationships were implicit rather than explicit recalled less of the total passage and fewer of the conditional relationships, though the recall of students from an ivy league university was not similarly affected. In another study (33) fifth grade subjects recalling causal relationships were more likely to recall the connected ideas than similar subjects who did not recall the causal relationships. Paris and Upton (48), in a study involving children in kindergarten through sixth grade, found that scores on questions dealing with intersentential inferences were the best predictors of free recall completeness. In contrast, Irwin (30) found that the recall of college students at a large midwestern university was not affected by the explicitness of connectives. Similar results were found by Roen (53). Taken together, these studies seem to indicate that connective explicitness is more likely to affect recall completeness for younger or lower ability readers.

Moreover, there is also evidence that connective concepts are often only implicitly stated in the textbooks for those readers. A study (16) comparing original passages with versions which had been made "easier" to read according to readability formulas revealed that the revised versions had more implicit and fewer explicit connectives. Similarly, Anderson, Armbruster, and Kantor (1) found serious coherence problems in an informal analysis of sixth grade science and social studies texts, many of which involved missing connectives. They speculate that this is the result of simplistic readability considerations in which connectives are omitted for the purpose of shortening sentences.

Irwin has investigated the hypothesis that lower level textbooks contained fewer connectives than higher level textbooks because of readability considerations. This hypothesis was not substantiated, but it was found that implicit connectives seem to be fairly common at all grade levels, at least in social studies texts, and the majority of these connectives express cause/effect relationships. (See Chapter 6.)

Finally, Irwin (31) and Irwin and Pulver (35) have found that third, fifth, eighth grade, and college level readers all seem to be less likely to comprehend causal relationships when they are stated implicitly rather than explicitly. In all of these studies, subjects reading social studies passages in which causal relationships were implicitly stated were less able to answer questions about the causal relationships than were the subjects reading the explicit versions. When combined with the results of the studies on recall completeness, this indicates that textbook writers should use caution when making connectives implicit.

Other Factors Possibly Related to Cohesion

Other research on discourse factors which can be conceptually related to the concept of cohesion also provides evidence that cohesion is related to comprehensibility. For instance, the "relational density hypothesis" (20) states that the probability of the recall of any idea is related to the number of other ideas in the text to which that idea is related. If this theory is correct, readers should remember highly cohesive texts in which, presumably, concepts are often repeated, better than less cohesive texts in which, presumably, concepts are not repeated often. This prediction has been supported by the results of two studies (20): In the first, relational density predicted the recall patterns written by college students immediately after reading; in the second, this hypothesis predicted oral recall patterns collected an hour after reading.

The compactness of subtopic structure has also been linked to recall completeness (2) and seems to be related to cohesion. Topical structure is defined as the "referential connections between statements in a paragraph in terms of each statement's reference to a main topic and subsets of statements to a specific subtopic" (p. 392). When subtopics occur consecutively, they are said to be compact. The alternative is a subtopic structure which is discontinuous. In a study involving sixth grade students, Aulls (2) found that a compact subtopic structure resulted in significantly more complete written free recall protocols for only those paragraphs which had been designed to be "meaningful," defined as consisting of familiar topics relating to the student's prior experience.

Finally, several studies have indicated that the presence of irrelevant information may interfere with comprehension. Thorndyke (57) found that presenting a condensed version of a news story in which irrelevant information was deleted resulted in better recall of the story than did presenting the entire story. Bruning (5) found that prompted recall of target sentences was greater when those sentences were presented in a relevant context than when they were in an irrelevant context. Rosenshine (54) reports that in a 1967 study by Funkhouser the presence of irrelevant information resulted in lower scores on related test items. Finally, Reder and Anderson (51) examined college students' literal and inferential comprehension of full and summarized passages and found a consistent advantage for the summary form after twenty minutes, one week, and six to twelve months, even when the main points were underlined in the full text. It could be hypothesized that in these studies irrelevant information in the full text reduced the number of cohesive relations between sentences.

Summary and Suggestions for Future Research

The results of research relating various cohesive relations to comprehension are consistent: A highly cohesive text is generally more comprehensible than one that is not very cohesive. All of the models of comprehension and inference seem to make the same assumption: Comprehension involves integrating a text into some sort of coherent semantic representation, and cohesive relations contribute to this. Moreover, these models predict that the processing demand of noncohesive texts seems to be related to inference. When a text lacks explicit links between sentences, a reader must infer those links.

Many of these theories make different assumptions regarding the exact nature of effective cohesive relations, though this question can be somewhat resolved by an examination of the available data. There seem to be at least three categories of cohesive relations which have been repeatedly identified in both linguistic theories and psychological studies.

First, some of the semantic relations between individual words as discussed in Halliday and Hasan (26) and van Dijk (60) have been examined in recent psychological research. In the Kintsch and van Dijk (40) data, this is limited to identical argument repetition, which would also include pronominal reference, but research indicates that other types of semantic relations, like entailment and presupposition, may also be related to comprehension (6, 23, 56). More research is needed to verify what types of specific semantic relations facilitate processing, and the relations specified by the linguists must each be investigated separately.

Second, it has been suggested that intersentential connectives add to the coherence of a text (6, 14, 26, 60). Only the explicitness of conjunctive relations has been verified as a relevant factor in psychological studies (32, 46, 48). More research is needed to determine what types of intersentential relations should be stated explicitly as well as what types facilitate comprehension.

Third, other syntactic markings based on the old-new information model, such as cleft and question constructions, also seem to contribute to comprehensibility (6, 10, 22). More of these structures should be examined, and it should be noted that a comprehension model based on the old-new hypothesis could also include the first two categories of relations (see 6).

Indeed, a synthesis of current approaches seems possible and should be investigated. Models of comprehension must account for all of the effects which have been verified, and there are many types of semantic relations which have not yet been adequately investigated.

The research relating cohesion to comprehension also has three direct applications to educational practice which merit investigation. First, the relationship of cohesion to the readability of instructional materials needs to be operationalized. In Chapter 1, Moe and Irwin suggest that teachers examine coherence links between main clauses in order to identify possible comprehension problems. In Chapter 3, Clark suggests a similar system using phrases and considering the variable of distance between referents. Approaches such as these should be extensively verified in instructional situations.

Second, developmental studies of children's ability to infer cohesive relations must also be conducted. Some available research results seem to indicate that students develop the ability to infer intersentential relationships as they mature (48) and that high ability readers may be more likely to make necessary intersentential inferences than low-ability readers, at least in the third grade (4). Interactive models of comprehension predict that poor readers who must devote more time and attention to lower level processes have fewer resources available for integrative processes (44, 55). Daneman and Carpenter (15) have also suggested that poorer readers may be using more of their working memory capacity for inefficient processing strategies and, therefore, may have less memory available for the storage functions necessary for integrative processes. A developmental model which relates the development of cohesion inference processes to the development of other reading skills would provide teachers with information about when students are ready to learn these skills.

Finally, the possibility of improving comprehension skills by providing guided practice in the inference of various cohesive relations must be investigated experimentally. If the inferring of these relations is an integral part of the comprehension process, then extensive training with questions focusing on the inference of cohesive relations might result in improved comprehension strategies. The growing body of evidence supporting the relationship between cohesion and comprehension suggests that this is a previously ignored or misunderstood comprehension skill.

References

1. Anderson, T.H., B.B. Armbruster, and R.N. Kantor. *How Clearly Written are Children's Textbooks? Or, of Bladderworts and Alfa*, Technical Report 16. Champaign: Center for the Study of Reading, University of Illinois, 1980.
2. Aulls, M.W. "Expository Paragraph Properties That Influence Literal Recall," *Journal of Reading Behavior*, 1975, 7, 391-400.
3. Barnitz, J.G. "Syntactic Effects on the Reading Comprehension of Pronoun-Referent Structures by Children in Grades Two, Four, and Six," *Reading Research Quarterly*, 1980, 15, 268-289.
4. Bridge, C., R. Tierney, and M. Cera. "Inferential Operations of Children Involved in Discourse Processing," paper presented at the National Reading Conference annual meeting, New Orleans, December 1977.
5. Bruning, R.H. "Short Term Retention of Specific Factual Information in Prose Contexts of Varying Organization and Relevance," *Journal of Educational Psychology*, 1970, 61, 186-192.
6. Carpenter, P.A., and M.A. Just. "Integrative Processes in Comprehension," in D. La-Berge, and S.J. Samuels (Eds.), *Basic Processes in Reading: Perception and Comprehension*. Hillsdale, NJ: Erlbaum, 1977.
7. Carpenter, P.A., and M.A. Just. "Reading Comprehension As Eyes See It," in M.A. Just and P.A. Carpenter (Eds.), *Cognitive Processes in Comprehension*. Hillsdale, NJ: Erlbaum, 1977.
8. Clark, C.H. "Assessing Comprehensibility: The PHAN System," *The Reading Teacher*, 1981, 34, 670-675.

9. Clark, H.H. "Bridging," in R. Schank and B. Nash-Webber (Eds.), *Theoretical Issues in Natural Language Processing.* Proceedings of the conference at the Massachusetts Institute of Technology, June 1975.

10. Clark, H.H. "Inferences in Comprehension," in D. LaBerge and S.J. Samuels (Eds.), *Basic Processes in Reading: Perception and Comprehension.* Hillsdale, NJ: Erlbaum, 1977.

11. Clark, H.H., and S.E. Haviland. "Comprehension and the Given-New Contract," in R.O. Freedle (Ed.), *Discourse Production and Comprehension: Volume 1.* Norwood, NJ: Ablex, 1977.

12. Clark, H.H., and C.J. Sengul. "In Search of Referents for Nouns and Pronouns," *Memory and Cognition,* 1979, *7,* 35-41.

13. Crothers, E.J. "Inference and Coherence," *Discourse Processes,* 1978, *1,* 51-71.

14. Crothers, E.J. *Paragraph Structure Inference.* Norwood, NJ: Ablex, 1979.

15. Daneman, M., and P.A. Carpenter. "Individual Differences in Working Memory and Reading," *Journal of Verbal Learning and Verbal Behavior,* 1980, *19,* 450-466.

16. Davison, A., R.N. Kantor, J. Hannah, G. Herman, R. Lutz, and R. Salzillo. *Limitations of Readability Formulas in Guiding Adaptations of Texts,* Technical Report 162. Champaign: Center for the Study of Reading, University of Illinois, 1980.

17. Entin, E.B., and G.R. Klare. "Factor Analysis of Three Correlation Matrices of Readability Variables," *Journal of Reading Behavior,* 1978, *10,* 279-290.

18. Fishman, A.S. "The Effects of Anaphoric References and Noun Phrase Organizers on Paragraph Comprehension," *Journal of Reading Behavior,* 1978, *10,* 159-167.

19. Frederiksen, C.H. "Inference and the Structure of Children's Discourse," paper for the symposium on the Development of Discourse Processing Skills, Society for Research in Child Development meeting, New Orleans, 1977.

20. Graesser, A.C. "How to Catch a Fish: The Memory and Representation of Common Procedures," *Discourse Processes,* 1978, *1,* 72-89.

21. Graesser, A.C., N.L. Hoffman, and L.F. Clark. "Structural Components of Reading Time," *Journal of Reading Behavior,* 1980, *19,* 135-151.

22. Grimes, J.E. *The Thread of Discourse.* The Hague, Netherlands: Mouton, 1975.

23. Haberlandt, K., and G. Bingham. "Verbs Contribute to the Coherence of Brief Narratives: Reading Related and Unrelated Sentence Triples," *Journal of Verbal Learning and Verbal Behavior,* 1978, *17,* 419-425.

24. Halliday, M.A.K. "Notes on Transitivity and Theme in English, Parts 1 and 2," *Journal of Linguistics,* 1967, *3,* 37-81, 199-244.

25. Halliday, M.A.K. "Notes on Transitivity and Theme in English, Part 3," *Journal of Linguistics,* 1968, *4,* 179-215.

26. Halliday, M.A.K., and R. Hasan. *Cohesion in English.* London: Longman, 1976.

27. Haviland, S., and H. Clark. "What's New? Acquiring New Information As a Process in Comprehension," *Journal of Verbal Learning and Verbal Behavior,* 1974, *13,* 512, 521.

28. Hayes-Roth, B., and P.W. Thorndyke. "Integration of Knowledge from Text," *Journal of Verbal Learning and Verbal Behavior,* 1979, *18,* 91-108.

29. Hildyard, A., and D.R. Olson. "Memory and Inference in the Comprehension of Oral and Written Discourse," *Discourse Processes,* 1978, *1,* 91-117.

30. Irwin, J.W. "The Effects of Coherence Explicitness on Mature Readers' Comprehension," *Journal of Reading Behavior,* 1982, *14,* 275-284.

31. Irwin, J.W. "The Effects of Explicitness and Clause Order on the Comprehension of Reversible Causal Relationships," *Reading Research Quarterly,* 1980, *15,* 477-488.

32. Irwin, J.W. "The Effects of Linguistic Cohesion on Prose Comprehension," *Journal of Reading Behavior,* 1980, *12,* 325-332.

33. Irwin, J.W. "Fifth Graders' Comprehension of Explicit and Implicit Connective Propositions," *Journal of Reading Behavior,* 1979, *11,* 261-271.

34. Irwin, J.W. "Implicit Connectives and Comprehension," *The Reading Teacher,* 1980, *33,* 527-529.
35. Irwin, J.W., and C. Pulver. "The Effects of Explicitness, Clause Order, and Reversibility on Children's Comprehension of Causal Relationships," *Journal of Educational Psychology,* 1984, *76,* 399-407.
36. Just, M.A., and P.A. Carpenter. "A Theory of Reading: From Eye Fixations to Comprehension," *Psychological Review,* 1980, *87,* 329-354.
37. Kintsch, W. "On Comprehension," paper presented at the annual meeting of the American Educational Research Association, San Francisco, 1979.
38. Kintsch, W. *The Representation of Meaning in Memory.* Hillsdale, NJ: Erlbaum, 1974.
39. Kintsch, W., E. Kozminsky, W.J. Streby, G. McKoon, and J.M. Keenan. "Comprehension and Recall of Text as a Function of Content Variables," *Journal of Verbal Learning and Verbal Behavior,* 1975, *14,* 196-214.
40. Kintsch, W., and T.A. van Dijk. "Toward a Model of Text Comprehension and Production," *Psychological Review,* 1978, *85,* 363-394.
41. Kintsch, W., and D. Vipond. "Reading Comprehension and Readability in Educational Practice and Psychological Theory," paper presented at the Conference on Memory, University of Uppsala, June 1977.
42. Klare, G.E. "The Measurement of Readability." Ames, Iowa: Iowa State University Press, 1963.
43. Lesgold, A.M. "Pronominalization: A Device for Unifying Sentences in Memory," *Journal of Verbal Learning and Verbal Behavior,* 1972, *11,* 316-323.
44. Lesgold, A.M., and C.A. Perfetti. "Interactive Processes in Reading Comprehension," *Discourse Processes,* 1978, *1,* 323-336.
45. Lesgold, A.M., S.R. Roth, and M.E. Curtis. "Foregrounding Effects in Discourse Comprehension," *Journal of Verbal Learning and Verbal Behavior,* 1979, *18,* 291-308.
46. Marshall, N., and M.D. Glock. "Comprehension of Connected Discourse: A Study into the Relationships between the Structure of Text and Information Recalled," *Reading Research Quarterly,* 1978, *1,* 10-56.
47. Moe, A.J. "Cohesion, Coherence, and the Comprehension of Text," *Journal of Reading,* 1979, *23,* 16-20.
48. Paris, S.G., and L.R. Upton. "Children's Memory for Inferential Relationships in Prose," *Child Development,* 1976, *4,* 660-668.
49. Petofi, J.S. "Beyond the Sentence, between Linguistics and Logic," *Style and Text.* Stockholm: Skriptor, 1975.
50. Reder, L.M. *Comprehension and Retention of Prose: A Literature Review.* Technical Report No. 108. Center for the study of Reading, University of Illinois at Urbana-Champaign, November 1978. (ED 165 114)
51. Reder, L.M., and J.R. Anderson. "A Comparison of Texts and Their Summaries: Memorial Consequences," *Journal of Verbal Learning and Verbal Behavior,* 1980, *19,* 121-134.
52. Riesser, H. "On the Development of Text Grammar," in W.U. Dressler (Ed.), *Current Trends in Textlinguistics.* New York: Walter de Gruyter, 1978.
53. Roen, D.H. "The Effects of Selected Textforming Structures on College Freshmen's Comprehension of Expository Prose." Ann Arbor, Michigan: University Microfilms International, 1981.
54. Rosenshine, B. "New Correlates of Readability and Listenability," in J. Allen Figurel (Ed.), *Reading and Realism.* Newark, DE: International Reading Association, 1969.
55. Stanovich, K.E. "Toward an Interactive Compensatory Model of Individual Differences in the Development of Reading Fluency," *Reading Research Quarterly,* 1980, *16,* 32-71.
56. Stone, V.F. "The Effect of Textual Cohesion on the Comprehension of Connected Discourse," paper presented at the annual meeting of the National Reading Conference, San Antonio, Texas, December 1979.

57. Thorndyke, P.W. "Knowledge Acquisition from Newspaper Stories," *Discourse Processes*, 1979, *2*, 95-112.
58. Thorndyke, P.W. "The Role of Inference in Discourse Comprehension," *Journal of Verbal Learning and Verbal Behavior*, 1976, *15*, 437-446.
59. Tierney, R.J., and J. Mosenthal. *Discourse Comprehension and Production: Analyzing Text Structure and Cohesion*, Technical Report 152. Center for the Study of Reading, University of Illinois at Urbana-Champaign, January 1980.
60. van Dijk, T.A. *Text and Context*. London: Longman, 1977.
61. Vipond, D. "Micro- and Macroprocesses in Text Comprehension," *Journal of Verbal Learning and Verbal Behavior*, 1980, *19*, 276-296.
62. Yekovich, F.R., and L. Manelis. "Accessing Integrated and Nonintegrated Propositional Structures in Memory," *Memory and Cognition*, 1980, *8*, 133-140.
63. Yekovich, F.R., C.H. Walker, and H.S. Blackman. "The Role of Presupposed and Focal Information in Integrating Sentences," *Journal of Verbal Learning and Verbal Behavior*, 1979, *18*, 535-548.
64. Yekovich, F.R., and C.H. Walker. "Identifying and Using Referents in Sentence Comprehension," *Journal of Verbal Learning and Verbal Behavior*, 1978, *17*, 265-277.

5

John G. Barnitz

The Anaphora Jigsaw Puzzle in Psycholinguistic and Reading Research

Recent developments on children's acquisition of reading have been influenced by research efforts in linguistics, psycholinguistics and cognitive psychology. Reading is viewed as a complex interaction of cognitive and linguistic processes with which readers construct a meaningful representation of the author's written message (26, 40, 53). In recent years much attention has been given to the role of text characteristics in reading (25, 35, 58). One aspect of text found to affect reading comprehension is *cohesion* (32), which is the set of elements which unify a text, allowing the ideas to "hang together" thereby facilitating comprehension (11). The most prolifically investigated cohesive device is the *anaphor,* which research has demonstrated strongly influences children's reading comprehension. Thus, it is important for reading teachers and researchers to understand the complexities of anaphoric comprehension in children's reading. (For a detailed description of anaphora, see Chapter 2 in this book.)

Sorting through the many research studies reminds me of assembling a large jigsaw puzzle with the thousand pieces scattered across various academic fields, with many pieces and the picture on the box missing. Furthermore, our understanding of much published research requires academic training in linguistics and experimental psychology. The following discussion is intended to assist reading educators in understanding some of the psycholinguistic research on pronoun reference, especially as it relates to children's reading comprehension.

A lengthy but partial list of references is also provided for researchers.

Anaphora and Cognition

Anaphoric resolution, or the process of determining the intended referent of an anaphoric form (*61*, p. 155), is an important property of the language/reading comprehension process (*18*). Moreover, because anaphoric comprehension involves many cognitive processes (such as language, inference, memory), it is important to understand some of the psychological studies on anaphoric processing.

Several important questions about the psycholinguistic processing of anaphora are relevant to understanding reading. How is anaphoric comprehension influenced by other language variables in a sentence or text? What is the role of the reader's or listener's prior knowledge in inferring a pronoun's referent? Do anaphoric structures influence reading or listening time? How is memory involved in the comprehension of pronouns?

Many linguistic variables in a sentence or discourse can affect the comprehension of pronouns. One study (*8*) documented that in complex cause-effect sentences with potentially ambiguous pronouns, verb properties can influence pronoun assignment. Compare the following two sentences:

(1) John telephoned *Bill* because *he withheld* some information.

(2) *John* telephoned Bill because *he wanted* some information.

Adults chose the preferred noun faster when the content of the subordinate clause was consistent with the "implied causality" bias of the verb as in sentence (2) above. Related studies by Garvey, Caramazza, and Yates (*24*) also showed that adults tended to choose an antecedent consistent with the main verb's implied bias, even though the pronoun is syntactically ambiguous.

(3) *George telephoned* Walter because *he* wanted sympathy.

(4) George *criticized Walter* because *he* wanted sympathy.

Thus, the verb tends to bias pronoun assignment in adult comprehension.

Gender clues also can be important in pronoun comprehension (*8*). For example, when the name *Mary* is substituted for *John* in examples (1) and (2), the reader will probably choose *Mary* for the pronoun *she*, as in examples (5) and (6):

(5) *Mary* telephoned Bill because *she withheld* some information.

(6) *Mary* telephoned Bill because *she wanted* some information.

Thus, gender agreement can serve as a clue for locating a referent for a pronoun.

In contrast to adults, middle and upper grade children tended to choose referents based on a strategy of parallel function. When given a choice between two referents in a preceding clause, readers often chose the referent in the same grammatical function (e.g. subject or object) (*24*). Thus, in examples (3) and (4), *he* would tend to be interpreted by children as referring to *George* because the two words function as subjects in paral-

helps explain why (subj) pronouns are easier

lel clauses. Sheldon (52) and Grober, Beardsley, and Caramazza (30) demonstrated that parallel function is one of the major "perceptual strategies" (5) used for comprehending sentences with potentially ambiguous pronouns in the subject position of subordinate clauses. Cowan (16), however, demonstrated the tendency for real world knowledge to override parallel function as in the following examples:

(7) Charles pulled the rug over to the *bookcase* and painted *it*.

(8) Maria placed the three sacks of flour beside the *carrots*, and then she washed *them*.

Thus, Cowan argued that more than one strategy may be operative in pronoun resolution. In selecting an antecedent for a pronoun, a reader can use strategies that involve parallel function and real world pragmatic knowledge. Thus, syntactic and pragmatic strategies interact in language comprehension.[2]

Indeed, the role of prior knowledge seems to be a crucial factor in the comprehension of pronoun-referent relations (49, 60, 61). Example (9) illustrates the role of prior knowledge in a reader's understanding of a pronoun's referent.

(9) I have a '71 Figeac, a '76 Fleurie, a '71 Ockfener Bockstein and a '75 Durkheimer Feuerberg in the cellar. Shall we have the German *ones* for dinner tonight?

This sentence clearly illustrates that the reader's prior knowledge, in this case of German wines, is crucial for inferring to which wines the pronoun *ones* refers.

In the psycholinguistic literature, a sufficient body of evidence illustrates that various language variables influence processing time. More specifically, several experiments have illustrated the effects of cohesion on comprehension by demonstrating that anaphoric resolution often requires additional processing time. For example, Garrod and Sanford (23) found that cohesion was related to processing time. Using sentences like

(10) A bus came roaring round the corner. The (vehicle/bus) narrowly missed a pedestrian.

they found that the reading time for adults was partially influenced by how semantically related the referents were. The repetition of *bus* required less time, while the word *vehicle*, which is not as closely related, took more processing time. McKoon and Ratcliff (45) similarly found that readers need extra processing time to make an inference based on prior knowledge of concepts and their lexical relationships.

Also affecting processing time for pronoun resolution are contextual constraints. Compare the following:

(11) John stood watching while Henry fell down some stairs. He ran for the doctor.

(12) John stood watching while Henry fell down some stairs. He thought of the future.

The target pronoun is more contextually constrained in the first sentence than in the second sentence. Hirst and Brill (*33*) found that processing sentences of the former type required less time than the second.

Another study that illustrates the interaction of anaphora and processing time is that of Clark and Sengul (*15*) who found that the syntactic distance between the pronoun and referent was related to processing time: Adults took less time when referents to noun phrases were one sentence or clause back than they took when the pronouns were further back in the text. Processing time effects can also be seen in the data presented by Ehrlich and Rayner (*20*): They found that adult readers spent more time reading the text *following* a pronoun when the referent was presented much earlier in the passage. Thus, anaphoric structures[1], combined with semantic and textual variables, have the potential for affecting the processing time.

Memory factors are also related to the comprehension of anaphora. Chafe (*9*) claimed that pronominalization can occur only if the referent is in the consciousness of the hearer or if it is previously understood information. In other words, if a pronoun refers to an antecedent that is in the working memory of the reader, then anaphoric resolution is more likely to occur. As mentioned above, Clark and Sengul (*15*) found that adult subjects required less time to comprehend sentences when the pronoun was located one sentence back than when it was located many sentences back. This also suggests the role of working memory in anaphoric processing.

Moreover, pronouns have a unifying effect on adults' recall of sentences. Lesgold (*41*) found that adults better recalled the content of clauses that were linked with a pronoun than content not linked by pronouns, indicating that pronouns force a unification of the semantic content in memory. On the other hand, he also found (*42*) that eight to ten year olds were less able to integrate information linked by pronoun-referent relationships. He suggested that young children have not yet totally developed the short term memory capacity for full integration of meaning linked by pronouns and referents. Thus, the development of pronoun comprehension skills may be strongly linked with the development of children's memory capacities.

The findings of the aforementioned linguistic and psychological studies are relevant to reading educators in demonstrating the complexities involved in anaphoric processing. It is no wonder that other studies on children's reading comprehension indicate that anaphoric structures are potential stumbling blocks for young readers. The remaining section reviews the findings of research studies on children's reading.[3]

Anaphora and Reading Skill Development

As children progress in their development of language and cognition, it is natural to expect an increase in their ability to comprehend pronouns. This prediction has been supported by various developmental reading studies, yet variations exist in some of the specific claims made by researchers.

For instance, while Barnitz (*1, 3, 4*) claimed that most pronoun-referent syntactic structures are comprehensible by sixth graders, Gottsdanker-Willekens (*29*) found that the number of pronouns in a passage significantly reduces eighth graders' comprehension. Moreover, as discussed earlier, various factors interact in anaphoric processing, further complicating research results. Reading researchers have clearly documented that several additional factors influence children's reading comprehension and recall of pronoun-referent structures: the type of anaphora, the type of antecedent, the direction of reference, the distance between pronouns and referents, and explicitness of reference. These, again, are interrelated in a passage and in the research studies, although they will be discussed separately.

One of the major questions reading educators ask is: Are certain types of anaphoric structures easier to comprehend than others? This is an important question, because the answer could affect curricular decisions about what structures should be mastered or taught at various grade levels. Bormuth, Carr, Manning, and Pearson (*7*) conducted the now classic study on fourth graders' comprehension of a wide variety of syntactic structures, including anaphora. They found that personal pronouns were easier for their subjects to comprehend than demonstrative noun phrase pronouns, which were easier than words referring to verbs (with *so*), which in turn were less difficult than words referring to clauses (with *so*). However, Lesgold (*43*) challenged this hierarchy by varying the semantic content of the passages and found a different hierarchy. Thus, the comprehensibility of a given anaphoric type may be strongly affected by such factors as passage content or the background knowledge of the reader.

Another study examining the effects of types of pronoun-referent structures is that of Barnitz (*1, 3, 4*), who found that children in grades 2, 4 and 6 generally recalled pronoun referents more frequently when the antecedent was a noun phrase than when it was a clause. The least difficult structures in this study tended to be intrasentential noun phrase structures in which the pronouns followed their antecedents, as compared to more difficult intersentential clausal pronominal structures.

More recent studies have also examined children's comprehension of various types of cohesive relations. Moberly (*46*) and Monson (*47*) investigated comprehension of the cohesive devices described by Halliday and Hasan (*32*). (See Chapters 1 and 2 in this volume.) Moberly compared the comprehensibility of four types of cohesive ties (reference, substitution, ellipsis, and lexical) by embedding them in two 800 word stories. She found that fourth and sixth grade children generally comprehend cohesion devices in the following order (from easiest to most difficult): reference, substitution, ellipsis, lexical. While this study demonstrates that elementary school children find some cohesive relationships in text more or less difficult than others, it also indicates that pronouns may not be as difficult as other types of cohesive relations.

In a related study (*47*), Monson compared the effects of the same cohesive types on the reading comprehension of children ranging from ages seven to twelve. Except for the seven year olds, the range (from easiest to most difficult) was found to be: reference, lexical, substitution/ellipsis. The data for the seven year olds in the study resulted in a different order of difficulty: lexical, reference, substitution/ellipsis. In addition, the order of referent and anaphor had a weak effect on recall; if the order was forward (antecedent-anaphor) the structures tended to be easier to recall than the reversed order (anaphor-referent).

These orders were illustrated by Barnitz (*1,3,4*) in examples (13) and (14) respectively:

(13) John wanted to buy a large *train set,* because *it* was on sale.

(14) Because *it* was on sale, John wanted to buy a large *train set.*

Barnitz (*1, 3, 4*) found that children in grades two, four, and six more frequently recalled a referent when the pronoun followed its antecedent than the reversed direction. Vietnamese high school students, likewise, more easily recalled referents that naturally preceded the pronoun, as compared to the reversed direction (*2*). Barnitz argued that this result is due to the fact that reversed directions are more complex syntactically and are more unnatural to children's experience with language. Finally, in her well-known oral language development study, Carol Chomsky (*13*) found that young children acquire backward pronominalization (anaphor-referent) after forward pronominalization (referent-anaphor), suggesting that order effects are operative in children's language development.[4]

Variation in the distance between the referent and anaphor may also influence children's reading performance. Dutka (*19*) argued that the distance an adult reader has to search for a referent is a good predictor of the potential difficulty of comprehending a pronominal structure. This appears to make sense in that the closer material holds a "privileged place in working memory" (*15*). However, Richek (*50*) found that the number of words between a pronoun and its referent (8-10 vs. 16-18) in short passages did not affect comprehension by third graders. Barnitz (*1, 3, 4*) also found that distance was not significant unless combined with other variables. However, the control for distance in Barnitz's project was weak, due to the short length of the passages. With Vietnamese high school students, Barnitz (*2*) did find that referent distance was a significant factor in recall after reading.

A more reliable study of the role of the distance variable is that of Moberly (*46*). While using longer passages, she found that the tie location was a significant variable in children's reading comprehension. Cohesive structures were generally better comprehended when the anaphor and referent were closer together than when they were farther apart. This finding is supported by psychological studies mentioned earlier (*15, 20*).

The presence or absence of part of the antecedent-anaphor relation can also affect children's comprehension. Richek (*50*) investigated the effects on third graders' reading of three structures embedded in short passages.

Noun: John saw Mary and *John* said hello to Mary.
Pronoun: John saw Mary and *he* said hello to her.
Null: John saw Mary and Ø said hello to her.

The null version was found to be less frequently recalled than the pronoun version, which in turn was less frequently recalled than the noun version.

A similar inference phenomenon was investigated by Stevenson (*55*). If the antecedent is not explicitly stated anywhere in the discourse, the reader will have to infer the referent from prior knowledge. Stevenson found that for both third and eighth grade students, scores for stated antecedents were significantly higher than scores for unstated antecedents.

Finally, the type of passage influences the comprehension of anaphoric relations. Kameenui and Carnine (*36*) found that when fourth graders read *narrative* passages, pronouns did not significantly affect their comprehension, but when they read *expository* passages, pronoun structures presented more difficulty than repeated nouns. Thus, Kameenui and Carnine argued that hierarchies of anaphoric structure difficulty must be interpreted in terms of additional text variables.

Teddlie (*57*) confirmed that global characteristics of connected discourse affected the anaphoric processing of children in grades two and four. On a cued recall task, but not on a free recall task, children were more successful recalling anaphoric relations that were related to the theme of a passage than those that were less central or important to the theme. Similarly, Frederiksen (*22*) claimed that high school students' comprehension of anaphora was sensitive to three major factors: the organization of ideas in the discourse, the surface syntactic structure, and the semantic content.

Thus, the study of anaphoric comprehension must be understood in the context of the interactive model of the reading process (*53*), which shows that various levels of language (discourse, syntax, semantics) and cognition (memory, inference, prior knowledge) interact simultaneously as the reader constructs a meaning for a passage. Indeed, any potential difficulties with comprehending anaphora may be due to all of these factors rather than to the pronoun. Pronouns are not necessarily the "villains" of reading comprehension, although experimental research may so imply.

A nonexperimental psycholinguistic study by Goodman and Gespass (*27*) recently challenged the instructional implications of the experimental psycholinguistic paradigm for investigating anaphoric comprehension. Objections raised by Goodman and Gespass included the fact that many experimental passages violate natural language constraints. Controlling various linguistic variables in short experimental passages is a difficult task. Further, many passages in various studies are shorter than most real life reading selections. Thus, children tested in experimental studies have fewer contextual clues for assigning reference. Using more natural passages, Goodman and Gespass found that children in grades two, four, and six made fewer miscues on pronouns than on other elements of discourse. They concluded that children have more control of cohesive relationships than previously realized. Goodman and Gespass argue that in the reading process, the reader expects texts to be cohesive and therefore infers anaphoric reference naturally. Thus, experimental findings, though useful in demonstrating the wide range of linguistic phenomena in reading, should be interpreted cautiously for any direct classroom application.

Summary and Recommendations

Psycholinguistic and educational studies have clearly shown that comprehending anaphora is a crucial part of the comprehension process. Several factors interact in determining whether a reader will comprehend and recall a given anaphor. These include specific passage content; passage type (expository vs. narrative); specific language structures (such as verb structure, parallel function, and pronoun gender); and finally, type, distance, direction and explicitness of reference. It is reasonable to conclude that processing difficulty or ease is a combination of all of these factors, not to mention other crucial reader characteristics like knowledge of passage content, memory development, inference ability, and linguistic development.

The phenomena discovered through experimental psycholinguistic research present useful information for teachers. Goodman and Gespass (27) recommend that teachers use natural cohesive texts in strategy lessons for complex anaphora. (See 28). Teachers can also use their theoretical knowledge of anaphora to provide students with experience in anaphoric resolution through the language experience approach or the directed reading-thinking activity (54). A teacher who finds that a particular child needs direct teaching may use some of the techniques recommended in Part Three of this book. Natural texts and tasks should be used whenever possible. In addition, activities for teaching comprehension of cohesion should not be isolated from the total text or total reading process.

Notes

[1] Note that in Chapters 1 and 2 structures in which the pronoun precedes the referent are called *cataphora*. In this chapter, the use of the term *anaphora* includes the idea of cataphora. That is, *anaphora*, as used in this chapter may denote a reference either for word or each word; the pronoun may precede or follow the referent.
[2] For additional studies involving the interaction of language variables, see Yekovich and Walker (64), Sheldon (52), and Wykes (63).
[3] Much more linguistic and psycholinguistic research has been conducted on anaphora. For more information on the linguistic aspects of anaphora, see Kantor (37), Barnitz (1), Webber (60, 61), and Kreiman and Ojeda (38). For discussions on children's early acquisition of the

pronoun system, see Huxley (*34*), Waryas (*59*), Chipman and DeDardel (*12*), Tanz (*56*), Flahive (*21*), Scholes (*51*), and Wykes (*63*). For discussion of the comprehension of pronouns by special needs children and adults, see Wilbur, Montanelli, and Quigley (*62*), Dalgleish and Enkelmann (*17*), and Grober and Kellar (*31*).

³See Bolinger (*6*) and Kuno (*39*) for theoretical discussions of backward pronominalization.

References

1. Barnitz, J.G. "Children's Development of Syntactic Aspects of Reading Comprehension: Pronoun-Referent Structures," unpublished doctoral dissertation, University of Illinois at Urbana-Champaign, 1978.
2. Barnitz, J.G. "Reading Comprehension of Anaphoric Syntactic Structures by Vietnamese Bilingual Students in High School," *Research on Reading in Secondary Schools: A Semiannual Report,* Monograph No. 7. Tucson: University of Arizona, 1981, 68-87.
3. Barnitz, J.G. *Reading Comprehension of Pronoun-Referent Structures by Children in Grades Two, Four, and Six,* Technical Report No. 117. Champaign: University of Illinois, Center for the Study of Reading, March 1979.
4. Barnitz, J.G. "Syntactic Effects on the Reading Comprehension of Pronoun-Referent Structures by Children in Grades Two, Four, and Six," *Reading Research Quarterly,* 1980, *15*, 268-289.
5. Bever, T.G. "The Cognitive Basis for Linguistic Structure," in J.R. Hayes (Ed.), *Cognition and the Development of Language.* New York: Wiley and Sons, 1970.
6. Bolinger, D. *Pronouns and Repeated Nouns.* Bloomington: Indiana University Linguistics Club, March 1977.
7. Bormuth, J., J. Carr, J. Manning, and P.D. Pearson. "Children's Comprehension of Between- and Within-Sentence Syntactic Structures," *Journal of Educational Psychology,* 1970, *61*, 349-357.
8. Caramazza, A., E. Grober, C. Garvey, and J. Yates. "Comprehension of Anaphoric Pronouns," *Journal of Verbal Learning and Verbal Behavior,* 1977, *16*, 601-609.
9. Chafe, W.L. "Language and Consciousness," *Language,* 1974, *50*, 111-113.
10. Chai, D.T. *Communication of Pronominal Referents in Ambiguous English Sentences for Children and Adults,* Report No. 13. Development of Language Functions: A Research Program Project. Ann Arbor: University of Michigan, January 1967.
11. Chapman, J. "Confirming Children's Use of Cohesive Ties in Text: Pronouns," *Reading Teacher,* 1979, *33*, 317-322.
12. Chipman, H.H., and C. DeDardel. "Developmental Study of the Comprehension and Production of the Pronoun 'It,' " *Journal of Psycholinguistic Research,* 1974, *3*, 91-99.
13. Chomsky, C. *The Acquisition of Syntax in Children from Five to Ten.* Cambridge: MIT Press, 1969.
14. Cirilio, R.K. "Referential Coherence and Text Structure in Story Comprehension," *Journal of Verbal Learning and Verbal Behavior,* 1981, *20*, 358-367.
15. Clark, H.H., and C.J. Sengul. "In Search of Referents for Nouns and Pronouns," *Memory and Cognition,* 1979, *7*, 35-41.
16. Cowan, J.R. "The Significance of Parallel Function in the Assignment of Intrasentential Anaphora," in J. Kreiman and A. Ojeda (Eds.), *Papers from the Parasession on Pronouns and Anaphora.* Chicago: Chicago Linguistic Society, 1980.
17. Dalgleish, B.W.J., and S. Enkelmann. "The Interpretation of Pronominal Reference by Retarded and Normal Readers," *British Journal of Educational Psychology,* 1979, *49*, 290-296.
18. Durkin, D. "What Is the Value of the New Interest in Reading Comprehension?" *Language Arts,* 1981, *58*, 23-43.
19. Dutka, J.T. "Anaphoric Relations, Comprehension, and Readability," in P.A. Kolers, M.E. Wrolstad, and H. Bouma (Eds), *Processing of Visible Language.* New York: Plenum Press, 1980.

20. Ehrlich, K., and K. Rayner. "Pronoun Assignment and Semantic Integration During Reading: Eye Movements and Immediacy of Processing," *Journal of Verbal Learning and Verbal Behavior,* 1983, *22,* 75-87.
21. Flahive, D. "The Development of Pronominalization in Children Five to Nine," paper presented at the Chicago Linguistic Society meeting, Chicago, 1976.
22. Frederiksen, J.R. *Understanding Anaphora: Rules Used by Readers in Assigning Pronominal Referents,* Technical Report No. 239. Champaign: University of Illinois, Center for the Study of Reading, 1982.
23. Garrod, S., and A. Sanford. "Interpreting Anaphoric Relations: The Integration of Semantic Information While Reading," *Journal of Verbal Learning and Verbal Behavior,* 1977, *16,* 77-90.
24. Garvey, C., A. Caramazza, and J. Yates. "Factors Influencing Assignment of Pronoun Antecedents," *Cognition,* 1976, *3,* 227-243.
25. Goetz, E.T., and B.B. Armbruster. "Psychological Correlates of Text Structure," in R.J. Spiro, B.C. Bruce, and W.F. Brewer (Eds.), *Theoretical Issues in Reading Comprehension.* Hillsdale, NJ: Erlbaum, 1980.
26. Goodman, K.S. "Reading: A Psycholinguistic Guessing Game," in H. Singer and R.B. Ruddell (Eds.), *Theoretical Models and Processes of Reading.* Newark, DE: International Reading Association, 1970.
27. Goodman, K.S., and S. Gespass. *Text Features as They Relate to Miscues: Pronouns,* Research Report No. 7. Program in Language and Literacy. Tucson: University of Arizona, Arizona Center for Research and Development, March 1983.
28. Goodman, Y.M., and C. Burke. *Reading Strategies: Focus on Comprehension.* New York: Holt, Rinehart and Winston, 1980.
29. Gottsdanker-Willekens, A.E. "The Interference of Some Anaphoric Expressions on Reading Comprehension," *Reading Psychology,* 1981, *2,* 132-145.
30. Grober, E.H., W. Beardsley, and A. Caramazza. "Parallel Function Strategy in Pronoun Assignment," *Cognition,* 1978, *6,* 117-133.
31. Grober, E., and L. Kellar. "Semantic Influences on Pronoun Assignment in Aphasia," *Applied Psycholinguistics,* 1981, *2,* 253-268.
32. Halliday, M.A.K., and R. Hasan. *Cohesion in English.* London: Longman, 1976.
33. Hirst, W., and G.A. Brill. "Contextual Aspects of Pronoun Assignment," *Journal of Verbal Learning and Verbal Behavior,* 1980, *19,* 168-175.
34. Huxley, R. "The Development of the Correct Use of Subject Personal Pronouns in Two Children," in G.B. Flores d'Arcais and W.J.M. Levelt (Eds.), *Advances in Psycholinguistics.* Amsterdam: North Holland, 1970.
35. Irwin, J.W. "The Effect of Linguistic Cohesion on Prose Comprehension," *Journal of Reading Behavior,* 1980, *12,* 325-332.
36. Kameenui, E.J., and D.W. Carnine. "An Investigation of Fourth Graders' Comprehension of Pronoun Constructions in Ecologically Valid Texts," *Reading Research Quarterly,* 1982, *17,* 556-580.
37. Kantor, R.N. "The Management and Comprehension of Discourse Connection by Pronouns in English," unpublished doctoral dissertation, Ohio State University, 1977.
38. Kreiman, J., and Ojeda, A.E. (Eds.). *Papers from the Parasession on Pronouns and Anaphora.* Chicago: Chicago Linguistic Society, 1980.
39. Kuno, S. "Three Perspectives in the Functional Approach to Syntax," in L.J. San and T.J. Vance (Eds.), *Papers from the Parasession on Functionalism.* Chicago: Chicago Linguistic Society, 1975.
40. Langer, J.A., and M.T. Smith-Burke (Eds.). *Reader Meets Author/Bridging the Gap.* Newark, DE: International Reading Association, 1982.
41. Lesgold, A.M. "Pronominalization: A Device for Unifying Sentences in Memory," *Journal of Verbal Learning and Verbal Behavior,* 1972, 316-323.
42. Lesgold, A.M. *Effects of Pronouns on Children's Memory for Sentences.* Development Center, University of Pittsburgh, 1972.

Barnitz

43. Lesgold, A.M. "Variability in Children's Comprehension of Syntactic Structures," *Journal of Educational Psychology,* 1974, *3,* 333-338.
44. Maratsos, M. "The Effects of Stress on the Understanding of Pronominal Coreference in English," *Journal of Psycholinguistic Research,* 1973, *2,* 1-8.
45. McKoon, G., and R. Ratcliff. "The Comprehension Processes and Memory Structures Involved in Anaphoric Reference," *Journal of Verbal Learning and Verbal Behavior,* 1980, *19,* 668-682.
46. Moberly, P.C. "Elementary Children's Understanding of Anaphoric Relationships in Connected Discourse," unpublished doctoral dissertation, Northwestern University, 1978.
47. Monson, D. "Effect of Type and Direction on Comprehension of Anaphoric Relationships," paper presented at the International Reading Association WORD Research Conference, Seattle, Washington, 1982.
48. Pearson, P.D., and D.D. Johnson. *Teaching Reading Comprehension.* New York: Holt, Rinehart and Winston, 1978.
49. Nash-Webber, B.L. *Inference in an Approach to Discourse Anaphora,* Technical Report No. 77. Champaign: University of Illinois, Center for the Study of Reading, January 1978.
50. Richek, M.A. "Reading Comprehension of Anaphoric Forms in Varying Linguistic Contexts," *Reading Research Quarterly,* 1977, *12,* 145-165.
51. Scholes, R.J. "Developmental Comprehension of Third Person Personal Pronouns in English," *Language and Speech,* 1981, *24,* 91-98.
52. Sheldon, A. "The Role of Parallel Function in the Acquisition of Relative Clauses in English," *Journal of Verbal Learning and Verbal Behavior,* 1974, *13,* 272-281.
53. Spiro, R.J., B.C. Bruce, and W.F. Brewer. (Eds.). *Theoretical Issues in Reading Comprehension.* Hillsdale, NJ: Erlbaum, 1980.
54. Stauffer, R.G. *The Language Experience Approach to the Teaching of Reading.* New York: Harper and Row, 1980.
55. Stevenson, J.A. "Effects of Explicit-Activated and Implicit-Activated Antecedents on Average Third and Eighth Grade Readers' Resolution of Anaphora," unpublished doctoral dissertation, University of Wisconsin at Madison, 1980.
56. Tanz, C. "Learning How *It* Works," paper presented at the Child Language Research Forum, Stanford University, April 1975.
57. Teddlie, J. "Discourse Effects on Children's Resolution and Recall of Anaphoric Relationships," unpublished doctoral dissertation, Texas Woman's University, 1979.
58. Tierney, R.J., and J. Mosenthal. "Discourse Comprehension and Production: Analyzing Text Structure and Cohesion," in J.A. Langer and M.T. Smith-Burke (Eds.), *Reader Meets Author/Bridging the Gap.* Newark, DE: International Reading Association, 1982.
59. Waryas, C.L. "Psycholinguistic Research in Language Intervention Programming: The Pronoun System," *Journal of Psycholinguistic Research,* 1973, *2,* 221-237.
60. Webber, B.L. *A Formal Approach to Discourse Anaphora.* New York: Garland Press, 1978.
61. Webber, B.L. "Syntax Beyond the Sentence: Anaphora," in R.J. Spiro, B.C. Bruce, and W.F. Brewer (Eds.), *Theoretical Issues in Reading Comprehension.* Hillsdale, NJ: Erlbaum, 1980.
62. Wilbur, R.B., D.S. Montanelli, and S.P. Quigley. "Pronominalization in the Language of Deaf Students," *Journal of Speech and Hearing Research,* 1976, *19,* 120-140.
63. Wykes, T. "Inference and Children's Comprehension of Pronouns," *Journal of Experimental Child Psychology,* 1981, *32,* 264-278.
64. Yekovich, F.R., and C.H. Walker. "Identifying and Using Referents in Sentence Comprehension," *Journal of Verbal Learning and Verbal Behavior,* 1978, *17,* 265-277.

6

Judith W. Irwin

Cohesion Factors in Children's Textbooks

Recent research in prose comprehension has repeatedly indicated a positive relationship between the "cohesion" of a text and its comprehensibility (*16, 19;* also see Chapter 4). For the purpose of the study reported in this chapter, *cohesion* is defined as the psychologically significant semantic links that tie individual sentences to adjacent sentences; this is to be distinguished from global unity achieved through a larger organizational pattern. According to most theories of linguistic inference, inferences are usually required (thereby increasing processing difficulty) when a text lacks these natural, explicit links between sentences (*3, 7, 27*). In addition, data on eye movement and reading time, showing extended processing time at the end of sentences, indicate that intersentential integration is an integral part of the comprehension process (*15*).

Lower level elementary textbooks have at least two characteristics which may reduce cohesion and, as a result, comprehensibility. First, in order to control readability, the sentences are purposely kept short, despite the fact that there is not much knowledge about how this is best accomplished. Second, many topics are treated briefly and superficially, probably for the purpose of keeping reading assignments short while covering a maximum number of basic concepts (*1*). Both of these characteristics may reduce natural cohesion.

Adapted from *Reading Psychology,* 1983, *4,* 11-23.

Thus, this study represents an initial investigation into the cohesion factors in instructional textbooks. The basic research questions could be stated as follows:

1) Are instructional textbooks written for the lower grade levels less cohesive than those written for higher grade levels?
2) What specific cohesion factors vary across the textbooks written for different grade levels?
3) What are the instructional implications of the varying cohesion factors?

Because this investigation was largely exploratory, specific hypotheses were not formulated.

Procedure

Materials

In order to limit the investigation to expository prose, only social studies textbooks were selected. For the initial analysis, one series was collected. However, the third and fourth grade texts in this series were composed of narrative material, and the eighth grade and high school level texts were not available, so substituting texts from another series was necessary. Additional texts were then randomly selected for grades 3, 5, and 8. Grades 3, 5, and 8 were chosen because they represented a period of transition from more controlled to less controlled vocabulary, sentence length, etc. Grades one and two were avoided because the many unnatural constraints on the language at those levels would make comparison and later substantive changes difficult.

The copyright data on all texts analyzed was no earlier than 1976, and the predicted readability level of the texts was checked using the Fry readability formula. All texts fell within the expected readability range for the given grade level. From each text, three 500-word samples were randomly chosen for analysis. None of these samples fell at the very beginning or end of the text.

Analysis Procedures

Because the actual processing order for individual propositions within clauses is difficult to specify and because the propositions within main clauses can easily be ordered into individual coherence graphs (19), only the "referential coherence" between main clauses was examined. (In terms of the Kintsch system of discourse analysis (17), two clauses are referentially coherent if they share a semantic argument.) All three 500 word samples from each text were, therefore, analyzed in terms of the number of instances in which a main clause did not share an argument with the preceding main clause.

The cohesion analysis system presented by Halliday and Hasan (9) was implemented directly. Because this analysis resulted in large scores, it was decided that reduced samples of only 300 words were sufficient for this analysis. In order to determine the importance of the variable of distance between tie members, an initial analysis was conducted for grades three and eight and the differences between the results for these grades were not judged consistent enough to warrant further analysis of this variable.

Finally, an extensive analysis of the connectives used was conducted for the same three 300 word samples from each text. The categories used in this analysis were based on the types of connective propositions described by Kintsch (17). In addition, the connectives were coded as to whether they were implicit or explicit and whether the connected concepts were within the same main clause (within-clausal) or in different main clauses (inter-clausal). A second rater analyzed a random sample from each of three grade levels (3, 5, and 8) in terms of all three of these analysis procedures. Inter-rater reliability coefficients for the shared argument measure, the cohesion analysis, and the implicit connective count were .98, .99, and .95 respectively.

Results

The results of the count of the number of instances in which adjoining main clauses did not share an argument are presented in Table 1. Both numbers of breaks and the average number of breaks in ten sentences are presented, because the number of sentences in the 1,500 words analyzed varied across the grade levels. A Kruskal-Wallis nonparametric analysis of variance revealed significant differences across grades three, five, and eight ($H = 5.75$ $p \leq .03$), the third grade texts clearly having fewer referential breaks than the other two grade levels.

Table 1
Referential Coherence Breaks between Main Clauses

Grade	Number	Breaks/10 Sentences
1	22	1.38
2	21	1.24
3	19 (16) (20)	1.34 (1.31) (1.39)
4	25	1.89
5	36 (28) (33)	3.03 (2.22) (2.46)
6-7	35	3.85
8	31 (29) (28)	2.90 (2.96) (2.53)
HS	35	4.32

Numbers in parentheses indicate the results from the second and third texts analyzed for that grade level.

Table 2
Number of Cohesive Ties in Each Main Category

Grade	Number of Sentences	Reference	Lexical	Conjunction	Ellipsis	Substitution	Total
1	142.5	112	350	13	4	4	483
2	115.5	157	314	32	16	0	519
3	84.5	148	218	27	10	1	404
		(145)	(221)	(42)	(5)	(1)	(414)
		(140)	(181)	(43)	(5)	(4)	(373)
4	81	160	206	47	7	3	423
5	79.5	143	184	27	10	1	365
		(138)	(200)	(29)	(2)	(1)	(370)
		(156)	(231)	(43)	(9)	(5)	(444)
6-7	45	124	156	39	10	1	330
8	62	117	175	42	0	0	334
		(97)	(198)	(54)	(2)	(2)	(353)
		(140)	(201)	(49)	(3)	(2)	(395)
HS	50.5	102	136	47	0	0	285

Numbers in parentheses indicate numbers found in the second and third texts analyzed for that grade level.

The results of the cohesion analysis are presented in Table 2. These results generally indicate that the language in the upper level books is less cohesive than that in the lower level books, though this trend was not statistically significant according to the nonparametric test for grades three, five, and eight. Though the samples from the high school text had only slightly more than half as many ties as the second grade samples, the multiple samples taken within grades three, five, and eight were not consistent within the grade levels and may indicate that texts within a readability range can vary widely in terms of these elements.

An examination of the trends in each category verifies intuitive predictions. The gradual decline in the reference category is due entirely to a decrease in the number of personal pronouns, which decreased from one in every ten words in the second grade text to one in every 75 words in the high school text in the initial analysis. The decline in the lexical category is due entirely to a decline in the number of exact reiterations, from one out of every three words in the first and second grade texts to one out of every nine words in the high school text. As would be expected, the number of conjunctions increases across the grades. However, Kruskal-Wallis tests revealed no significant differences between grades three, five, and eight on any of the individual cohesive tie types, and again, an examination of the data reveals large inconsistencies within grade levels.

The use of ellipsis in lower level texts raises some substantive questions. Ellipsis may be used in the lower grades to keep the sentences short, but it is possible that young students may have trouble inferring the omitted item. Indeed, clausal ellipsis is more common than nominal or verbal ellipsis, so a reader must usually infer entire propositions.

It is also interesting that the general distribution across types of ties within each of these books remains fairly constant in spite of the varying totals. For instance, in the grade two book, 30 percent of the ties were referential, 60 percent were lexical, 4 percent were conjunctive, 4 percent were ellipsis, and 0 percent were substitution. In the fifth grade book, 40 percent were referential, 50 percent were lexical, 7 percent were conjunctive, 3 percent were ellipsis, and 0 percent were substitution. These distributions are similar to those found in an earlier study (12) and may reflect a natural language constraint which should be investigated further.

When the cohesion results are viewed in terms of the number of ties per sentence, they appear quite different, as would be expected as a result of the varying sentence length. The number of referential ties per sentence seems to go up in the higher grades (from .79 in grade one to 2.02 in high school), while the number of lexical ties per sentence remains constant (2.57 grade one, to 2.69 in high school). The number of conjunctive relationships per sentence moves from almost none in the first grade textbook (.09), which seems unnaturally low, to almost one in every sentence in the high school textbook (.93).

Table 3
Explicit Connectives

Grade	Within Sentence											Intersentential											Total
	Cj	D	Ca	P	Csn	Ct	Cnd	T	L	M	Total w/in	Cj	D	Ca	P	Csn	Ct	Cnd	T	L	M	Total I-S	
1	5	1	0	0	0	11	0	3	7	2	29	2	0	0	0	1	2	0	2	0	0	7	36
2	11	2	2	19	1	10	0	14	26	0	85	4	0	0	1	4	0	1	7	1	0	18	103
3	15	3	0	20	2	20	0	13	42	0	115	6	1	3	8	2	7	2	4	2	0	35	150
3b	23	8	0	14	2	4	0	18	3	1	73	4	0	1	9	2	0	1	1	0	0	18	91
3c	19	1	3	4	0	4	0	9	0	3	43	0	0	0	0	1	1	0	9	0	0	14	57
4	23	4	0	5	9	19	3	17	31	0	111	5	1	2	1	1	0	0	2	4	1	15	126
5	12	4	1	1	1	5	0	5	22	0	51	6	0	1	4	3	1	0	5	7	1	32	83
5b	15	2	0	7	3	5	6	22	43	2	102	4	0	5	7	0	0	0	4	1	0	16	118
5c	12	1	0	5	0	2	1	20	32	4	80	11	0	0	1	4	2	2	7	1	0	30	110
6-7	10	2	1	3	2	3	1	15	21	0	58	17	0	4	0	3	2	1	10	8	1	45	103
8	17	0	0	11	3	4	0	10	14	0	59	14	2	3	15	1	0	0	4	3	0	44	103
8b	28	3	5	9	6	18	0	23	16	0	108	2	0	2	10	6	1	1	1	1	0	20	128
8c	20	1	1	5	0	6	0	24	29	2	88	9	0	4	0	6	2	1	8	0	0	29	117
HS	8	2	0	6	2	6	0	6	15	0	45	21	1	2	6	6	4	0	7	6	0	53	98

Cj - Conjunction   Ct - Contrast
D - Disjunction   Cnd - Conditional
Ca - Cause   T - Time
P - Purpose   L - Location
Csn - Concession   M - Manner

Table 4
Implicit Connectives

Grade	CA		P	CSN	CT	CND	Total
	C→	E→C					
1	1	0			2		3
2	5	2		1			8
3	5	5	3		1		14
							(1)
							(7)
4	8	4	1	1	3		17
5	7	3			1		11
							(10)
							(3)
6-7	5	3	1				9
8	7	5		3	1		16
							(6)
							(11)
HS	6	8		2			16

Numbers in parentheses indicate the results of the analysis of the second and third texts at the grade level.
C→E – implicit causal with cause stated first
E→C – implicit causal with effect stated first

Finally, the results of the explicit connective analysis are presented in Table 3. A dramatic increase in the total number of connectives present occurs between the first and second grade texts, but the numbers seem reasonably similar across the grades after this. When multiple samples were examined for grades three, five, and eight, a Kruskal-Wallis test revealed no significant differences among these grades for within-sentence connectives, for intersentential connectives, or for the total number of connectives. Initial analysis indicated a shift from primarily within-sentence connectives to intersentential connectives occurring at around the fifth grade level, but in some of the other texts, this shift is not as dramatic. Further investigation revealed that the sentence length in the texts showing fewer intersentential connectives is shorter than in the texts showing more intersentential connectives.

The numbers of implicit connective relationships found in the text samples are presented in Table 4. In the second grade text, there is almost one in every one hundred words, and in the fourth grade text this number is almost twice as high. No significant differences were found among the texts from grades three, five, and eight using the Kruskal-Wallis test, but, again, there seems to be considerable variance within grades in terms of this variable. Finally, most of the implicit connectives seem to be causal relationships, and they are often presented in the presumably more difficult effect-cause order.

Discussion

Overall, the results of this analysis of selected social studies textbooks did not substantiate the prediction that that limited sentence and text length resulting from readability considerations also results in less cohesion in lower level textbooks. Indeed, in terms of the frequency of shared arguments across main clauses, lower level textbooks seem to be more cohesive than upper level textbooks. Moreover, in terms of the total numbers of cohesive ties, connective concepts, and implicit connectives, no significant differences across the selected grade levels were found. Perhaps this indicates that textbook writers at all three of these levels are equally constrained by readability formulas. For instance, though sentences need not be as short in eighth grade books as in third grade books, the eighth grade ideas are more complex and limiting sentence length may result in the type of artificiality found in third grade texts. An alternative conclusion might be that these texts retain a natural level of cohesion in spite of readability constraints. Further analyses of natural language and of other textbooks are needed to resolve this question.

Another important result of this study is the amount of variance found within the selected grade levels. One cause of this might be the unavoidable variance in topics. In addition, different authors may be more or less sensitive to these variables when writing. Whatever the cause, the implication is that there is no consistent relationship between traditional readability and explicit or implicit connectives or between traditional readability and cohesive elements.

Moreover, several questions are raised by the shared argument analysis results. One might ask if students are being adequately prepared to deal with the lack of referential cohesion in the upper level texts, which is evidenced by the fact that there are more than four breaks in every ten sentences in the high school samples analyzed. The effectiveness of direct instruction in the inference of cohesive links merits further investigation. This might be given during the transition period which seems to fall in the intermediate grades and might facilitate children's comprehension of the increasingly less cohesive textbook language. In addition, comprehension in the upper grades might be improved by making the language in these textbooks more cohesive in terms of shared arguments.

The results of the cohesion analysis raise at least one contrasting question. Lower level books may be *too* cohesive for effective processing strategies. The extremely high numbers of exact reiterations in the lower level books, probably a result of vocabulary constraints, clearly account for a large part of their cohesion. Excessive use of exact word repetition presents at least two possible problems (26): It reduces natural redundancy in which the use of different words provides two ways of viewing the same topic, and 2) it results in the imprecise use of the reiterated words, resulting in a lack of clarity.

The large numbers of implicit causal relationships found in some of these textbooks also have important instructional implications. Research indicates that even college students may have trouble inferring implicit causal relationships *(11)*. Further research should be conducted to determine what types of implicit causal relationships are or are not comprehended by children of various ages. For now, teachers should be aware of these relationships so that they can point them out to students, and textbook writers might consider paying closer attention to explicit statements of causal relationships.

References

1. Anderson, T.H., B.B. Armbruster, and R.N. Kantor. *How Clearly Written Are Children's Textbooks? Or, Of Bladderworts and Alfa,* Technical Report 16. Champaign: Center for the Study of Reading, University of Illinois, 1980.
2. Carpenter, P.A., and M.A. Just. "Integrative Processes in Comprehension," in D. La-Berge and S.J. Samuels (Eds.), *Basic Processes in Reading: Perception and Comprehension.* Hillsdale, NJ: Erlbaum, 1977.
3. Crothers, E.J. *Paragraph Structure Inference.* Norwood, NJ: Ablex, 1979.
4. Davison, A. *Readability — Appraising Text Difficulty,* Technical Report 24. Champaign: Center for the Study of Reading, University of Illinois, 1981.
5. Davison, A., R.N. Kantor, J. Hannah, G. Hermon, R. Lutz, and R. Salzillo. *Limitations of Readability Formulas in Guiding Adaptations of Texts,* Technical Report 162. Champaign: Center for the Study of Reading, University of Illinois, 1980.
6. Fishman, A.S. "The Effects of Anaphoric References and Noun Phrase Organizers on Paragraph Comprehension," *Journal of Reading Behavior,* 1978, *10,* 159-167.
7. Frederiksen, C.H. "Inference and the Structure of Children's Discourse." Paper for the Symposium on the Development of Discourse Processing Skills, Society for Research in Child Development meeting, New Orleans, 1977.
8. Graesser, A.C., N.L. Hoffman, and L.F. Clark. "Structural Components of Reading Time," *Journal of Verbal Learning and Verbal Behavior,* 1980, *19,* 135-151.
9. Halliday, M., and R. Hasan. *Cohesion in English.* London: Longman, 1976.
10. Hildyard, A., and D.R. Olson. "Memory and Inference in the Comprehension of Oral and Written Discourse," *Discourse Processes,* 1978, *1,* 91-117.
11. Irwin, J.W. "The Effects of Explicitness and Clause Order on the Comprehension of Reversible Causal Relationships," *Reading Research Quarterly,* 1980, *15,* 477-488.
12. Irwin, J.W. "The Effects of Linguistic Cohesion on Prose Comprehension," *Journal of Reading Behavior,* 1980, *4,* 325-332.
13. Irwin, J.W. "Fifth Graders' Comprehension of Explicit and Implicit Connective Propositions," *Journal of Reading Behavior,* 1979, *11,* 261-271.
14. Irwin, J.W. "Implicit Connectives and Comprehension," *The Reading Teacher,* 1980, *33,* 527-529.
15. Just, M.A., and P.A. Carpenter. "A Theory of Reading: From Eye Fixations to Comprehension," *Psychological Review,* 1980, *87,* 329-354.
16. Kintsch, W. "On Comprehension." Paper presented at the annual meeting of the American Educational Research Association, San Francisco, 1979.
17. Kintsch, W. *The Representation of Meaning in Memory.* Hillsdale, NJ: Erlbaum, 1974.
18. Kintsch, W., E. Kozminsky, W.J. Streby, G. McKoon, and J.M. Keenan. "Comprehension and Recall of Text as a Function of Content Variables," *Journal of Verbal Learning and Verbal Behavior,* 1975, *14,* 196-214.
19. Kintsch, W., and T.A. van Dijk. "Toward a Model of Text Comprehension and Production," *Psychological Review,* 1978, *85,* 363-394.

20. Kintsch, W., and D. Vipond. "Reading Comprehension and Readability in Educational Practice and Psychological Theory." Paper presented at the conference on Memory, University of Uppsala, June 1977.
21. Lesgold, A.M. "Pronominalization: A Device for Unifying Sentences in Memory," *Journal of Verbal Learning and Verbal Behavior,* 1972, *11,* 316-323.
22. Lesgold, A.M., S.R. Roth, and M.E. Curtis. "Foregrounding Effects in Discourse Comprehension," *Journal of Verbal Learning and Verbal Behavior,* 1979, *18,* 291-308.
23. Marshall, N., and D. Glock. "Comprehension of Connected Discourse: A Study into the Relationships Between the Structure of Text and Information Recalled," *Reading Research Quarterly,* 1978, *1,* 10-56.
24. Paris, S.G., and B.K. Lindauer. "Constructive Aspects of Children's Comprehension and Memory," in R.V. Kail and J.W. Hagen (Eds.), *Perspectives on the Development of Memory and Cognition.* Hillsdale, NJ: Erlbaum, 1977.
25. Paris, S.G, and L.R. Upton. "Children's Memory for Inferential Relationships in Prose," *Child Development,* 1976, *47,* 660-668.
26. Shuy, R.W., and D.L. Larkin. "Linguistic Considerations in the Simplifications/Clarification of Insurance Policy Language," *Discourse Processes,* 1978, *1,* 305-321.
27. Thorndyke, P. "The Role of Inference in Discourse Comprehension," *Journal of Verbal Learning and Verbal Behavior,* 1976, *15,* 437-446.
28. Vipond, D. "Micro- and Macroprocesses in Text Comprehension," *Journal of Verbal Learning and Verbal Behavior,* 1980, *19,* 276-296.
29. Yekovich, R.F., and C.H. Walker. "Identifying and Using Referents in Sentence Comprehension," *Journal of Verbal Learning and Verbal Behavior,* 1978, *17,* 265-277.

Part 3
Teaching Cohesion Comprehension

7

Cynthia J. Pulver

Teaching Students to Understand Explicit and Implicit Connectives

Many students seem to have difficulty understanding what they read. One possible reason for this difficulty is that they do not understand the meaning and purpose of connectives. The purpose of a connective is to enable the reader to find the conceptual relationships between the ideas and events expressed in the text. Sometimes the connective will be explicitly stated, as in sentence (1).

(1) John came home from school, *after* Mary came home from school. In order to understand this sentence, the reader must recognize that "after" is a connective denoting time sequence and that it indicates a specific conceptual relationship. Unfortunately, students often ignore even explicitly stated connectives (*10*). For instance, after reading sentence (1), many students believe that John came home before Mary, because John is mentioned first.

Moreover, even though many students have trouble understanding sentences with explicit connectives, many authors choose to leave out the connectives. The reader must then infer the implicit connective. For example, students reading sentences (2) and (3) in a history textbook would need to be able to infer that (2) is causally related to (3).

(2) Mexico allowed slavery.

(3) Many Americans moved there.

Irwin (Chapter 6 herein) has found that implicit connectives seem to be fairly common in textbooks for all grade levels, yet Irwin and Pulver (*9*) have found that many students do not make these necessary inferences. Several recent studies, however, indicate that the ability to infer connectives may be enhanced through instruction (7, 5).

In this chapter, I will suggest some general procedures for teaching connective comprehension and describe some activities that have proven effective in helping students understand connectives (11). Since many students have difficulty understanding explicit connectives as well as implicit connectives, the activities begin with teaching the comprehension of explicit connectives, followed by suggestions for teaching the comprehension of implicit connectives. The final section of the chapter suggests methods to assess a student's ability to comprehend connectives. A sample test that assesses comprehension of implicit causal relationships is also provided.

General Tips for Teaching Connective Comprehension

General procedures involved in connective comprehension instruction include identifying common connectives and selecting which type to teach, teaching the skill before assigning an activity, watching for ambiguous connectives, selecting appropriate materials, using the students' prior knowledge, and sequencing the lessons effectively.

Identifying Common Connectives

In order to teach your students to understand connectives, you must be able to identify the connectives commonly found in the materials they read. The table on page 69 provides a list of ten common connective concepts. It also includes some of the cues used to signal the connective relationship. You will probably need to study this table before teaching connective comprehension.

Be selective. It may be difficult to decide which of the ten major classes of connectives to teach. You should be selective: Teach those connectives that may cause difficulty for your students in their daily assignments. For example, while reading social studies materials, students must be able to understand causal relationships. First, determine whether your students are having difficulty understanding causal relationships. If they are, then instruction on that topic is in order.

Teach. Durkin (4) found that there is remarkably little direct comprehension instruction, though many educators agree that it would probably be useful (3). In a useable model for directly teaching comprehension, Irwin (8) suggests that comprehension skill instruction include any or all of the following.

Explication: Directly explaining the skill to the students.

Modeling: Orally modeling the skill by describing one's own thought processes.

Questioning: Asking questions that encourage students to model or describe the skill, while using it with actual materials.

Some Common Types of Connective Concepts

Types	Cues Used	Example
Conjunction	and in addition to also along with	Jack went to the store. Sally went also.
Disjunction	or either... or...	Either Jack went to the store, or he went home.
Causality	because so consequently	Jack went home because he was sick.
Purpose	in order to for the purpose of so that	Jack went home in order to get his money.
Concession	but although however yet	Jack left for home, but he hasn't gotten there yet.
Contrast	in contrast similarly (also comparative and superlative forms of adjectives)	Jack was very sick. In contrast, I feel better!
Condition	If...then... unless except	If Jack is sick, then he can't play ball.
Time	before always after while when from now on	Before Jack got sick, he went to the store.
Location	there where	Jack is at home, There, he will be able to rest.
Manner	in a similar manner like as	Jack was blue and feverish, as Sally was yesterday.

From J.W. Irwin, *Teaching Reading Comprehension Processes*. Englewood Cliffs, NJ: Prentice-Hall, 1986. Used with permission.

Activity: Practice activities.
This is similar to the four stage instructional model provided by Baumann and Stevenson (see Chapter 9), in which instruction is construed to consist of 1) an introduction/example, 2) direct instruction, 3) teacher-directed application, and 4) independent practice. Whichever model they use, teachers using the activities described in this chapter should realize that several kinds of direct teaching procedures should precede the assignment of individual practice activities.

Watch for ambiguity. While giving instruction concerning connectives, you must be aware that connectives may be ambiguous. Some connectives have multiple meanings. In sentence (4) the connective "so" is expressing causality. In sentence (5) "so" is expressing purpose.

(4) Mary had the flu, so she had to stay home from school.

(5) Mary went to school so she could learn to read.

Students should be instructed to identify the author's intended meaning by using the clues in the context. For example, read sentence (6).

(6) As John was coming home, Mary left for work.

It can be interpreted to mean that Mary left for work *while* John was coming home or that Mary left for work *because* John was coming home. If the next sentence in the paragraph were (7) below, the reader might infer "while," if the next sentence were (8) the reader would probably infer "because."

(7) They accidentally met in the hallway.

(8) She did not want to see him.

Prior knowledge. Students should also be instructed to use their knowledge of the topic when they are trying to understand connectives and the related events. [(9) provides an example.]

(9) Gold was discovered in Alaska. Many Americans traveled there. The reader probably has some knowledge of this topic. For example, the reader may know that

1. Gold is valuable.
2. People want gold, because it is valuable.
3. A discovery of gold might cause people to travel to Alaska.

This knowledge would clearly help the reader to understand the implicit causal relationship between the two sentences in (9). Encourage students to think about what they already know about the topic as they read.

Appropriate materials. It has already been mentioned that you should look at daily reading assignments when selecting which connective to teach. Similarly, daily assignments probably provide the best materials for teaching connective comprehension. If your students are having difficulty understanding causal connectives while reading social studies materials, then you should use social studies materials to teach these connectives. The instruction should evolve so that the students can apply their new knowledge concerning connected events to current reading assignments.

The materials must be at the students' instructional reading level. If the materials are too difficult, the students will probably not comprehend the explicit or the implicit connectives.

Lesson sequence. A final consideration in designing activities is the sequence of lessons. The activities suggested in this chapter were developed so that the more concrete concepts are presented first. Initial activities should probably deal with the concrete, everyday experiences about which students have more prior knowledge. You can also order lessons according to potential difficulty by first presenting explicit connectives in sentences and passages. After the students understand explicitly stated relationships, delete the connectives and have students supply them in a modified cloze procedure. Then you can present activities in which the connectives are stated implicitly, first in sentences and then in whole passages.

Suggested Activities

In the examples below, the subject matter is social studies, and the connective concept used is causality. These activities can, however, be adapted for any kind of material and for any type of connective. Keep in mind that you should present the activities to the students by introducing explicit connectives before implicit connectives, and by presenting activities dealing with everyday experiences before presenting the connectives in subject matter materials.

Understanding Explicit Connectives

Sentence completion. Teach students to recognize connectives as "signals" for specific relationships by having students complete sentences. For example, in the following sentences, they must determine the possible causes for the effects:

1. The tire on my bike is flat, because....
2. The flower died, because....
3. The car would not start, because....
4. There was a flood, because....

Discuss the students' endings: Are they all causes? Is there more than one correct answer? Then, have the students determine possible sentence endings for less concrete relationships. For instance, you might use the following sentences:

5. I decided to study for the test, because....
6. I gave my mother a big hug, because....
7. I like my best friend, because....
8. Sometimes I get angry at my friend, because....

Have students note that each phrase they had to complete began with a connective. In this case, "because" signaled that the next part of the sentence would tell the cause, or what made the first event happen.

When teaching about causality, you may want to continue with similar activities in which "so" expresses the relationship. In this case, "so" signals the effect rather than the cause. For instance, you might use the following:

1. Mike tied Sam's shoelaces together, so....
2. Lightning struck the old tree, so....
3. There was too much heavy, wet snow on the roof of the house, so....
4. Bill was really bored during math class, so....

Again, discuss the endings created by the students. Have students note that each phrase they had to complete ended with "so," and that "so" signaled that the next part of the sentence would tell the effect.

Explicit connectives presented in subject area sentences. After students understand explicit connectives in everyday experiences, introduce them to explicit connectives in the subject area materials. You may want to tell your students that these relationships are commonly found in this particular subject area and that if they understand these relationships, reading books in this subject area will be easier for them.

Below are some examples of explicitly stated relationships typical of social studies books:

1. The soil was rich in the West, so many pioneers decided to move there.
2. Columbus sailed west to reach the east, because he believed that the world is round.
3. Because runaway slaves could travel only at night, they decided to rest during the day.
4. The war was called a "world war" because it spread all over the world.
5. The Indians believed that animals had magic powers, so they did religious dances to honor them.
6. The French and the Indians were friends because they had to work together.
7. Many Europeans came to America because they could practice their religion here.
8. Many people support the Equal Rights Amendment, because they believe that women should have the same rights that men have.

Ask the students questions based on these relationships. Have them note the "signal" words and review what these signals mean.

Explicit connectives presented in subject area passages. When the students understand explicit connectives in subject area sentences, you can use subject area passages. The following examples have been adapted from a social studies text (6):

1. The Mississippi River became a major water highway. Hundreds of steamboats carried goods and passengers up and down the river. The steamboat captains had to be very skilled, because the Mississippi was full of sandbars (adapted from page 256).

2. In December of 1620 the Mayflower sailed into the harbor at Plymouth, and anchored a mile off shore. No homes had been built in Plymouth yet, so the Pilgrims decided to live on the ship. Each day those who were not ill rowed ashore to work. First they built a Common House—a large shed to be used as headquarters. Then they built a storehouse and a house for the sick (adapted from page 120).

Pulver

3. Sitting Bull was born near the Black Hills of South Dakota. He was a Sioux Indian. To the Sioux, the Black Hills was a holy place. A treaty made in 1868 granted this land to the Sioux forever, so no whites were ever to go there. But in 1872, whites poured into the area looking for gold (adapted from page 210).

Begin by having students identify the relationship by looking for the explicit connectives. Then ask the students questions based on the relationship. Use a similar procedure for each passage. You may vary this procedure by having the students make up a question based on the relationship, after you have given them the answer.

Selecting Appropriate Connectives

Selecting appropriate connectives for sentences. In this activity students select appropriate connectives for sentences in which the connectives have been deleted. Present sentences with missing connectives. Have the students determine which connectives would make sense. One way to do this is to present sentences visually, on the chalkboard or an overhead. Give the students response cards on which the connectives have been written. Each student will have a card for each connective under study. As the sentence is presented, the students must hold up the card(s) containing the appropriate connective(s).

Sample sentences:
1. I'm going to a party after school, _____ I hope the day goes by quickly.
2. The car would not start, _____ it ran out of gas.

Selecting appropriate connectives for implicit relationships found in subject area sentences and passages. This activity is similar to the preceding activity, except that sentences are taken from subject area materials. The students must also select appropriate connectives for passages as well as sentences.

Use the same procedure as in the previous activity, or have students write their answers in the corresponding blanks.

Sample sentences:
1. The farmers wanted to take land from the Indians, _____ it was good for raising crops.
2. Jefferson wanted to know what the West was like, _____ he asked Lewis and Clark to explore.

Sample passages:
1. According to the legend, Juan Ponce de León was looking for a "fountain of youth," _____ he had heard that its waters would make old people young again. In 1513 he explored the coast of Florida, which he thought was a large island. He did not realize that he was the first Spaniard to reach North America (adapted from *1*, p. 114).

2. Slavery in the Americas grew, _____ the plantations needed many workers. At first, the Spanish tried to force Indians into slavery. This did not work, _____ they brought in slaves from Africa. By 1600 there were 40,000 black slaves in Spanish America (Adapted from *1*, p. 127).

Clause Combining

Matching clauses. This activity can help students understand how clauses can be combined to create a sentence containing a connective. Provide the students with sets of clauses that could be combined, written on pieces of paper. One of the clauses should contain an explicit connective.
Samples:
Physical

My bike is rusty,	so I will have to paint it.
This tree will fall down soon,	because I have almost chopped through the trunk.

Psychological

Frank thinks that insects are really interesting,	so he is going to study them for his science project.
The old house was dark and spooky,	so Alice knew she didn't want to go inside.

Have students match the clauses to make complete sentences that make sense. Then ask students questions based on the relationships.

Combining clauses. In this activity, students combine clauses with a connective to create a sentence. For causal relationships, the selection of the appropriate connective is related to clause order, as in the following:

This milk tastes terrible, because it is sour.
It is sour, so this milk tastes terrible.

This is not true for all connective relationships, so be careful.

Present two clauses, neither containing an explicit connective, written on separate strips of paper. Have the connectives on separate strips. Discuss the students' knowledge of the topic to help them determine the cause and the effect. Then have students combine the clauses with an appropriate connective. Have the students compare their sentences. Are they all the same? Discuss how the clauses could be combined in different ways.

Continue by having the students randomly draw cards with connectives written on them. Students must use the connectives from the cards to combine the clauses. Discuss the results.

As a final activity, you may want to present sentences on the chalkboard or overhead. Have the students orally switch the clause order and change the connective.

Implicit Connectives in Whole Passages

In this activity students learn a strategy to help them determine the implicit connective relationships in a whole passage. Discuss with the students the fact that connectives are often not stated directly. Present a passage with one implicit relationship. Discuss ways students can determine whether an implicit relationship is being presented, and how to determine the appropriate connective.

Students should be taught to do the following:

1. Look at where the sentences come together; think about how the sentences are related to one another.
2. Think about what they already know about the topic, as an aid in determining the relationship.
3. Try to insert a connective between two sentences that contain related events. Does the new sentence make sense?

Sample passage:

> In the southern colonies, farming was most important. The main crops were rice, tobacco, and indigo, which is a plant used to make a blue dye. These crops were grown mostly on plantations. Many people were needed to do the work on the plantations. Indentured services were brought from Europe (adapted from *1*, pp. 140-141.)

You may want to have the students fill out a worksheet similar to the one that follows.

Write the two sentences that make up the causal relationship:

1. *Many people were needed to do the work.*
2. *Indentured servants were brought from Europe.*

Now combine these sentences into one sentence using a "signal" word.

Many people were needed to do the work, so indentured servants were brought from Europe.

Make up a "why" question about this causal relationship.

Why were indentured servants brought from Europe?

Applying What Has Been Learned to a Current Reading Assignment

Discuss the fact that students should apply what they have learned to reading their texts. As a group, read a passage from a current assignment that contains an explicit relationship. Discuss the topic of the passage. Have students determine the relationship and answer a question based on it. Use the same procedure with another passage containing an implicit relationship. Next, give the students a copy of part of their next reading assignment. Have them mark all of the implicit relationships by directing them to "see how many you can find." Have them make up questions based on five of these relationships. Finally, have the students take turns asking the questions they have made up. As you go through the assignment, identify and discuss the implicit relationships.

Incidental Teaching of Connective Inference

You may not feel that a systematic approach like the one described in this chapter is necessary for your class. You can still reinforce this skill in specific assignments. Once you are aware of the types of connective concepts your students encounter in their reading, you can make sure that they understand those concepts. Ask questions about the connective relationships, and discuss their meaning during regular class discussions. Before giving an assignment, make sure that your students have sufficient background knowledge about the topic. This will greatly increase their understanding of the implicit connective relationships.

Diagnosis

When you are diagnosing a student's comprehension of connectives, you must first determine whether the text is at an appropriate reading level. You can assess this by constructing questions about specific facts in the passage. A student who is unable to answer factual questions will probably not be able to draw the appropriate inferences.

The student having difficulty comprehending the connectives in materials at an appropriate reading level may lack prior knowledge about the topic. Thus, you may wish also to ask questions designed to assess the student's prior knowledge. Finally, if the student can understand the facts and has adequate prior knowledge but does not make the appropriate connective inferences, instruction is in order.

A sample test. You can diagnose a student's comprehension of connectives with an informal test. A sample test that has been checked for reliability and validity is included at the end of this chapter (see *11*). This sample test assesses a fifth grade student's comprehension of implicit causal relationships. Since causal relationships are common in social studies materials, the passages were taken from a social studies textbook. The passages all contain one or two implicit causal relationships. During field testing, short answer questions were found to be the most reliable. Therefore, the questions for each passage are in the short answer format. One question deals with each causal relationship stated in the passage. There are also two fact questions and two prior knowledge questions for each passage.

To construct a similar test, first select passages that contain the connective relationships you want to assess. Then write short answer questions about the connective relationships. You should also include some fact and prior knowledge questions. Make sure that each question has only one right answer. If the student is able to answer most of the fact and prior knowledge questions but has difficulty with the questions concerning the connective relationships, instruction is probably needed.

Summary

Many students have difficulty understanding what they read. One reason some students have difficulty is that they do not understand the connective relationships, especially when they are only implicitly stated.

Although the ability to understand implicit relationships may be related to age or reading ability, it may be enhanced through instruction (5, 7, 11).

There are ten common types of connective relationships (8), and you may wish to become familiar with those your students will encounter in their reading. In teaching your students about connectives, you must remember to be selective, use direct instruction, watch for ambiguous connectives, make sure your students have sufficient prior knowledge about the topic, and select appropriate materials.

A systematic approach to the teaching of connectives is also provided in this chapter. The initial activities deal with concrete concepts, the final activities with implicit connectives in content area materials. If such a systematic approach is not appropriate for your students, you may want to reinforce this skill when it comes up in a specific assignment. You may also want to construct a test for your students to determine who needs instruction. A sample test for fifth grade students concerning implicit causal relationships in social studies materials is provided.

Appendix

SAMPLE TEST
Implicit Causal Relationships
in
Social Studies Materials

Name	Date

Read each passage, then answer the questions that come after it. You will find the answers to the questions under "According to the passage..." in the passage. The answers to the "Do you know?" questions are *not* in the passage. See if you can think of the answers to those questions. You will read and answer questions for five passages.

(Note: In the final version of this test each set of questions should be on a separate page immediately following the appropriate passage. Students should not look back at the passage while answering the questions.)

Roads

The first settlers who moved west traveled mainly on trails left by the Indians. These trails were not wide enough or strong enough for the heavy wagons of the settlers. Many private companies began to build new roads.

A toll, or fee, was charged when travelers used the road. The company needed help to pay for the road. When the travelers approached a new section of road, a toll-taker would collect the travelers' money. Then, the travelers would go on down that stretch of road.[1]

According to the passage
1. Why were the new roads built?
2. When was a toll charged?
3. Who made the trails that the settlers traveled on at first?
4. When was a toll, or fee, charged?
   Do you know?
5. Today, what type of road do travelers have to pay to use?
6. Where in the United States did the settlers go if they wanted to find rich farm land?

---

[1]Adapted from J. Allen, *Americans*. New York: Litton, 1979, 199-200.

Lafayette

During the Revolutionary War, several American officers were from Europe. Lafayette was an affluent Frenchman. He believed in the Americans' fight for freedom and admired their courage. He wanted to help them.

Lafayette made plans to sail to America to join Washington. The king of France told Lafayette to stay in France. He had not yet decided to help the Americans.

But Lafayette had made up his mind. He bought a ship and kept it hidden in a Spanish harbor. He escaped from France dressed as a poor messenger. He went to Spain and sailed to America. Lafayette became a general and served without pay.[2]

According to the passage
1. Why did Lafayette want to help the Americans?
2. What country did Lafayette come from?
3. Why did the king of France tell Lafayette to stay in France?
4. How did Lafayette dress to escape from France?
   Do you know?
5. What country did the Americans fight during the Revolutionary War?
6. What country did France help during the Revolutionary War?

---

[2]Adapted from *Our Country* of Tiegs-Adams: Our Land and Heritage series. Copyright 1979 by Ginn and Company. Used with permission.

Puritans

The Puritan leaders made everyone in the Puritan colony of Massachusetts go to the Puritan church. Many people had come to America to practice religion in their own way. They did not want to go the Puritan church.

Roger Williams was a Puritan minister. He had to leave Massachusetts. He did not think that everyone should have to go to the Puritan church. In 1636, he started a settlement which he called Providence. It came to be known as Rhode Island. There, people could practice religion in their own way.[3]

According to the passage
1. What was the name of the Puritan colony?
2. Why didn't some people want to go to the Puritan church?
3. What colony did Providence become?
4. Why did Roger Williams have to leave Massachusetts?
   Do you know?
5. What is a colony?
6. Which Massachusetts settlement was founded by the Pilgrims?

[3]Adapted from Allen, *Americans*, p. 126.

Reaper

Grain grew well in the Middle West. The soil was fertile and the land was flat. While harvesting, the farmers had to walk through the field, cutting the grain with sharp blades. Then they had to go back, gather the grain, and tie it into bunches. This was slow, hard work.

In the 1830s, an inventor named Cyrus McCormick made a machine he called a reaper that was pulled by horses. As its blades turned, they could cut five times as much grain as could be cut by hand.[4]

According to the passage
1. Who invented the reaper?
2. Why did the grain grow well?
3. Where did the grain grow well?
   Do you know?
4. What crop was the reaper probably used to harvest?
5. What is fertile soil?

[4]Adapted from Allen, *Americans*, p. 212

Explicit and Implicit Connectives

Indians

The Indians used to roam over vast plains hunting for food. When they were forced to live on the reservation, life was completely different for them. United States soldiers made them live in a fairly small place which they could not leave.

The land on the reservations was too dry to farm. They could not raise enough to eat. The government promised to give them food and supplies. The government agents often cheated the Indians out of these goods. The Indians needed these goods to survive.[5]

According to the passage
1. Why was life completely different for the Indians on the reservations?
2. Why couldn't the Indians raise enough food to eat?
3. How were the Indians used to getting their foods?
4. Who cheated the Indians?
   Do you know?
5. Whey were the Indians forced to live on reservations?
6. What does "vast" mean?

---

[5]Adapted from Allen, *Americans,* pp. 259-260.

References
1. Allen, J. *Americans.* New York: Litton Educational Publishing, 1979.
2. Brown, G.S. *Our Country.* Lexington, MA: Ginn, 1979.
3. Duffy, G.C., and L.R. Roehler. "The Illusion of Instruction," *Reading Research Quarterly,* 1982, *17,* 438-445.
4. Durkin, D. "What Classroom Observations Reveal About Reading Comprehension Instruction," *Reading Research Quarterly,* 1978-1979, *4,* 481-533.
5. Gordon, C.J. "The Effects of Instruction in Metacomprehension and Inferencing on Children's Comprehension Abilities," doctoral dissertation, University of Minnesota, 1980. *Dissertation Abstracts International,* 1980, *41*(3), 1004-A.
6. Gross, H., D. Follett, R. Gabler, W. Burton, and B. Ahlschwede. *Exploring Our World: The Americas.* Chicago: Follet, 1977.
7. Hansen, J. "The Effects of Inference Training and Practice on Young Children's Reading Comprehension," *Reading Research Quarterly,* 1981, *16*(3), 391-417.
8. Irwin, J.W. *Teaching Reading Comprehension Processes.* Englewood Cliffs, NJ: Prentice-Hall, 1986.
9. Irwin, J.W., and C.J. Pulver. "The Effects of Explicitness, Clause Order, and Reversibility on Children's Comprehension of Causal Relationships," *Journal of Educational Psychology,* 1984, *76,* 399-407.
10. Nicholson, T., and R. Imlach. "Where Do Their Answers Come From? A Study of the Inferences Which Children Make When Answering Questions About Narrative Stories," *Journal of Reading Behavior,* 1981, *13*(2), 111-129.
11. Pulver, C.J. "The Effects of Small Group and Computer Assisted Inference Training Programs on Fifth Grade Students' Comprehension of Implicit Causal Relationships," unpublished doctoral dissertation, Purdue University, 1983.

8

Anne E. Gottsdanker-Willekens

Anaphoric Reference Instruction:
Current Instructional Practices

This chapter examines current instructional practices for helping readers comprehend anaphoric structures and summarizes the types of activities that have been used. Basal reading and language arts texts and college textbooks for teachers are examined in terms of the types of instruction suggested. Specific activities from basal series are also presented.

Research on Anaphora and Reading Comprehension

Researchers agree that pronouns and other anaphoric structures affect reading comprehension and, furthermore, that this effect is age-related. Difficulties in comprehension of pronouns and other referent structures have been noted in children through grade eight.

In a now classic study, Bormuth, Manning, Carr, and Pearson (6) found that fourth grade students had difficulty comprehending 14 different types of anaphoric structures, with comprehension varying from 64 percent to 86 percent correct. Although Lesgold challenged the results of that study on the basis of uncontrolled semantic factors, he too found comprehension of third and fourth grade students on the same 14 structures to range between 54 percent and 91 percent correct (27).

When looking specifically at pronouns, Richek (35, 36) found that third grade students had difficulty understanding pronoun paraphrases. Furthermore, Gottsdanker-Willekens (20) found that eighth grade students had difficulty comprehending passages that contained many pronouns; this indicates that a high frequency of pronoun usage may lead to difficulties in reading comprehension.

In another study focusing on pronouns, Chai (7) observed a developmental increase in ability to resolve pronominal ambiguities. (Students were fifth, seventh, and eighth graders and college students.) Barnitz (5) also found a developmental change in ability to comprehend pronoun referent structures in grades two, four, and six, with students in the higher grades having higher comprehension scores. Thus, there does seem to be agreement that children in grades two through eight have difficulty comprehending anaphora (6, 20, 27, 35, 36) and that the ability to comprehend these structures increases developmentally (5, 7).

A number of recent studies have looked at comprehension of anaphora from the perspective of cohesive and lexical ties (see Chapter 4), since anaphora serve a cohesive function. From that viewpoint, cohesive and lexical ties may improve a text's comprehensibility, but the ability to comprehend these ties may increase developmentally.

Use of cohesive ties within text does appear to affect a text's comprehensibility. Irwin (22) had college students read one of two versions of a passage, one with twice as many cohesive ties as the other. She found that the higher cohesion level positively affected both the ease of comprehension (calculated as reading time per 100 propositions recalled) and memory stability (measured by a delayed prompted recall task). Irwin also found that subjects were more likely to be able to summarize the high cohesion level passage than the low cohesion level passage. Thus, increased use of ties appeared to increase a passage's comprehensibility.

Chapman (9) also found that the use of cohesive ties influenced a text's comprehensibility. Comparing 15 year old students' comprehension of two versions of a text (isolated sentence version or tied version), Chapman observed that "a good proportion of the gain in scores comes from the presence of the cohesive tie relationship when the tie extends to more than one sentence" (p. 14).

In looking at comprehension of lexical ties as a developmental issue, Moberly (28) found sixth grade students more able than fourth grade students in comprehension of reference, substitution, ellipsis, and lexical ties in immediate, mediated, and remote locations. Monson (30) also observed developmental differences between children aged seven to eight, eight to nine, and nine to ten, in comprehension of referents, backward referents, substitution ties, and ellipses. Finally, Chapman (8) noted that nine and ten year olds performed better on cloze tests that deleted four different types of ties (reference, substitution, conjunction, and lexical cohesion) than did six and seven year olds.

From these studies, it appears that the use of lexical and cohesive ties affects a text's comprehensibility (9, 22) and that the ability to comprehend these ties improves developmentally (8, 28, 30). It seems important, then, that instructional materials and practices guide the reader in comprehending these relationships. The next step is to look at current instructional techniques and materials to see if this is indeed the case.

Theory into Practice: Reading and Language Arts Texts

I have examined basal reading and language arts texts to determine the extent to which the topic of anaphoric relations in general, and pronouns specifically, was covered. In this informal survey, I used the following series and levels. (Unfortunately, not all levels of each basal series were available.)

A. Scott, Foresman, *The New Open Highways* (*23*)
   Grades 1, 2, 3, 4, 5, 6
   Scott, Foresman, *Scott, Foresman Reading* (*1*)
   Levels 1, 2, 3, 4, 5, 6, 7, 8, 9, 10, 11
B. Harcourt Brace Jovanovich, *The Bookmark Reading Program*, second edition (*16*).
   Levels 1, 2, 3, 4, 5, 6, 7, 8, 9, 10, 11, 12
C. Ginn, *Ginn Reading 360 Program* (*11*)
   Levels 3, 4, 5, 6, 7, 8, 9, 10, 11, 12
   Ginn, *Ginn Reading 720 Program*
   Levels 3, 8, 11, 13, 15
D. Harper and Row, *Harper and Row Design for Reading* (*31*)
   Levels 11, 13, 17
E. American Book Company, *American Book Reading Program* (*24*)
   Levels A, B, C, D, E, F, G, H, I, J, K, L, M
   Skills Books, Levels I, J, K, L, M, N
F. Rand McNally, *Rand McNally Reading Program: Young American Basic Series* (*18*)
   Levels 1, 2, 3, 4, 5, 6, 7, 8, 9, 10, 11, 12
G. Holt, *The Holt Basic Reading System* (*17*)
   Levels 1, 2, 3, 4, 5, 6, 7, 8, 9, 10, 11, 12, 13, 14, 15
H. Merrill, *The Merrill Linguistic Reading Program* (*32*)
   Levels A, B, C, D, E, F, G, H, I, J, K
   Spirit Masters Reinforcement Materials Books, Levels F, G, H

Only those series containing some instruction concerning comprehension of pronouns are reported in this survey.

Durkin (*14*, p. 24) found "surprisingly little space...assigned to anaphora" in basal reader manuals. In a content analysis of five basal reader series (*13*), Durkin found that none of the texts surveyed deals with all five of the topics she identified that pertained to anaphora, "even though anaphoric devices cause comprehension problems" (p. 30). As might be expected, the current investigation found that different series showed considerable variation in the types of anaphoric structures selected for instruction, in the objectives for this instruction, in the types of instructional procedures and activities used, and in the suggestions for follow up instruction.

In the series with the least amount of instruction, comprehension of anaphoric relations (specifically pronouns) was viewed as a vocabulary activity. The series that did refer to use of syntactic and semantic clues to aid comprehension rarely informed either the teacher or the students what clues, such as gender or singular or plural markers, were available to the reader and how to use those clues. Pragmatic clues tended to be omitted entirely in all the series examined, when students should have been encouraged to use their social knowledge of how the world operates in determining the likelihood of a derived interpretation of text. In addition, there was little explanation for the teacher of how to remediate students' problems in assigning referents. The occasional reinforcement activities tended to provide only further practice rather than additional instruction.

The types of pronouns presented for instruction in these series are shown in Table 1. The types of pronouns ranged from personal pronouns only, to personal, possessive, and demonstrative pronouns, to personal, reflexive, and relative pronouns. As can be seen in Table 1, all series did cover personal pronouns, and one series briefly looked at "unusual" pronouns—*thou, thee, thy* and *thine.* These categories of pronouns were not always named and differentiated within the basal; frequently different types of pronouns were all classified simply as pronouns, and sometimes the categories had another name, such as "common" pronouns.

Table 1
Pronouns Taught in the Basal Series

Basal Series	Personal pronouns	Demonstrative pronouns	Possessive pronouns	Reflexive intensive pronouns	Relative pronouns	"Unusual" pronouns
A	X					
B	X	X	X			
C	X					
D	X			X	X	
E	X		X			
F	X		X		X	X
G	X		X			
H	X					

A. Scott, Foresman (*1, 23*)
B. Harcourt Brace Jovanovich (*16*)
C. Ginn (*11*)
D. Harper and Row (*31*)
E. American Book (*24*)
F. Rand McNally (*18*)
G. Holt (*17*)
H. Merrill (*32*)

Gottsdanker-Willekens

The categories for instruction also varied widely among the different basals, with pronouns being subsumed under categories as general as Language Development, Language Extension, Language/Mechanics Skills, and Vocabulary Skills, or as specific as Syntactical Understanding or Using Context to Determine Word Referents. Only one of the basals surveyed included pronoun referent resolution as a comprehension skill; the others presented it as a language skill. The descriptive term used by any given series seemed to indicate the approach used: Developmental (indicated by *language development*), Skills (indicated with the word *skills*), or Linguistic (as indicated by *syntactical understanding*).

Finally, the given objectives also varied. Some instructional objectives were defined as follows: Recognizing (or identifying) Pronoun Referents, Using Pronouns to Replace Nouns, Substituting Pronouns for Nouns, Finding Antecedents of Pronouns, and Using Synonyms and Pronouns to Avoid Repetition of a Noun. Some objectives were extremely specific, asking students to "use semantic and syntactic context clues to determine which word or words in given sentences underlined pronouns stand for."

Activities Used for Teaching the Comprehension of Anaphoric Structures

A variety of activities have been suggested to help students learn about pronouns and how to comprehend pronoun referent structures. Using an expanded version of Barnitz's classification (4) of sentence comprehension techniques (which discusses paraphrases, cloze, text manipulation, and sentence building and sentence combining techniques for comprehension of all types of sentence structures), I devised the following categories for pronoun comprehension activities. All of the activities included here were found in the basal series examined, but only a few types accounted for most of the activity. The most frequently encountered types of activities are marked with asterisks.

Clozelike Techniques

Written activities, referent deleted.

1. In written text, referents are deleted within the text. They are supplied in a list or in multiple-choice format. The student fills in the blank with the correct referent. Example:

When _____ went to the store, she bought some candy.

Tom   Suzy   Mom and Dad

Directions to the student: Circle the word that belongs in the blank.

2. In written text, some referents and some pronouns are deleted and listed on the page; the student fills in the blank with the appropriate referent or pronoun.

3. In written text containing pronouns that are numbered and underlined, the student supplies the referent on the correspondingly numbered blank line.

Written activities, pronoun deleted.

*1. In written text, pronouns are deleted. The student fills in the blank with the appropriate pronoun.

2. In written text, pronouns are deleted. They are supplied in a list or multiple-choice format. The student selects the appropriate pronoun. Example:

When Suzy went to the store, _____ bought some candy.

    he   it   she

Directions to the student: Circle the word that belongs in the blank.

3. The teacher puts on the board a sentence containing blanks for pronouns and displays a set of pronoun word cards. The student selects the appropriate pronoun word cards to fill in the blanks and then circles the antecedent.

4. In written text, referents are underlined and spaces left blank for pronouns. The student supplies the appropriate pronoun.

5. In written text, pronouns are deleted and variant forms are supplied. The student supplies the correct pronoun.

Oral activity.

The teacher reads a story aloud, pausing at pronouns. Students supply the correct pronouns from a list on the board.

Modifications and Manipulations of Text, Written and Oral Activities

1. Given a paragraph (or sentence) with no pronouns, the student rewrites it with pronouns.

2. A sentence or paragraph is given with nouns to be replaced either underlined or italicized. Example:

Suzy went to play with Michelle.

Directions to the student: Replace the italicized words with pronouns.

3. A sentence or paragraph is given in which the student is to replace the nouns with pronouns from a list provided.

4. Given a passage with many pronouns, the student reads aloud or rewrites the passage, replacing pronouns with the appropriate referents. (Variations: The pronouns may be underlined; the passage may contain only a few pronouns.)

*5. As in 4, but the student substitutes pronouns for all referents (written).

6. As in 4 above, with the referents underlined and pronouns supplied.

*7. As in 4, 5, and 6, in an oral activity.

8. The teacher puts on the board a sentence containing pronoun word cards. Students substitute word cards bearing their names for the pronoun word cards; then they stand in front of their names.

Paraphrase techniques, written and oral activities

1. Given at least three different versions of a text, the student selects equivalent paraphrased versions. (Variation: The student selects the non-equivalent paraphrased version.) Example:

Version I   Tom and Jane went to the zoo. Then he went   home.
Version II   Tom and Jane went to the zoo. Then they went home.
Version III   Tom and Jane went to the zoo. Then Tom went home.

Question for student: Which two versions mean the same thing?

2. Given at least two different versions of a text, the student detects and explains meaning changes evident in the different versions.

3. Given two versions of a text, one with pronouns and one without, the student compares how the different versions sound. (Variation: The student decides which version sounds better.)

Pronoun Referent Assignment Techniques, Written Activities

*1. In written text containing both pronoun and referent, the student identifies (circles or underlines) both of these structures. (Variation: Only the pronoun or only the referent is to be identified.)

2. In written text containing both pronoun and referent, the student writes the same number over the corresponding pronoun and referent.

3. In written text containing both pronoun and referent, the student draws an arrow from the pronoun to the referent (or from the referent to the pronoun). (Variation: A list of pronouns and referents follows the text, and the student matches corresponding pairs.)

4. In written text containing both pronoun and referent, the student lists both of these structures, telling how they agree in number and gender.

5. In written text containing both pronoun and referent, the teacher underlines the referent and the student underlines the pronoun. (Variation: The teacher underlines the pronoun and the student underlines the referent.)

6. In written text containing underlined referents and blanks for pronouns, the student supplies the pronouns. (Variation: Student supplies the referent.)

7. In written text containing both pronoun and referent, and with the pronoun listed below the text, the student supplies the referent corresponding to the pronoun listed. (Variation: referents listed below; student selects the appropriate referent.)

8. In written text containing incorrect usage of a pronoun, the student detects the incorrect usage and rewrites the sentence correctly. (Variation: Rewrite only.)

9. In written text containing incorrect usage of a pronoun, the student selects the pronoun from a list (or from multiple-choice alternatives).

Questioning Techniques, Written and Oral activities

*1. Students identify referents through discussion.

Anaphoric Reference Instruction

2. The teacher asks questions requiring the student to know to whom or what the pronoun refers.

3. The student tells to whom or what the pronoun refers.

*4. The teacher asks to whom or what the pronoun refers. Students respond and explain how they knew the answer.

5. The student identifies the pronoun and the word in the main clause to which it is related.

6. The teacher asks the student to recall the antecedent of a pronoun.

7. The teacher underlines the pronoun, and the student identifies the antecedent.

8. The teacher underlines the pronoun, leads the students to define the referent, asks each student to guess the referent and explain that choice, and has the class vote for the correct referent. The teacher then gives the correct answer and explains why it is correct.

9. The student identifies the speaker in a passage.

10. After reading a passage, the student is asked to figure out who is telling the story and to identify the clues used in determining the speaker.

11. In written text containing ambiguous pronoun reference, the student discusses and rewrites to clarify. (Variation: Rewrite only.)

Writing and Speaking Applications
Writing activities
1. The student uses pronouns in written sentences.

2. The student writes a paragraph and checks for pronoun and referent agreement.

Speaking activities
1. The student uses pronouns in oral sentences.

2. Guessing game: The teacher makes a statement using pronouns, and the students identify the person or thing to which the pronouns could refer. (Variation: A student makes up the same type of statement, and other students guess the referent.)

Theory into Practice: Teacher Preparation Methods Texts

Current college textbooks convey little information regarding instruction about pronouns and other types of anaphoric structures. In a survey of over 60 reading and language arts methods texts published between 1975 and 1982, I found only 7 books dealing with pronoun comprehension. By far the most complete coverage was in Pearson and Johnson's *Teaching Reading Comprehension* (*33*), which described a variety of types of anaphoric structures and suggested instructional activities. The coverage of the Pearson and Johnson text and the other six texts is summarized in Table 2.

The Pearson and Johnson text provided a theoretical discussion and detailed description of many types of anaphoric structures, as well as several types of activities for instruction and reinforcement of comprehension of pronoun referent assignment. The Aulls text (3) also informed the reader about comprehension of pronouns, with several types of activities represented, including one based on the cloze procedure. The remainder of the college texts examined that did include some information regarding comprehension of pronouns contained surprisingly little information concerning how to teach comprehension of pronouns; furthermore, the authors totally omitted discussion of other types of referent structures. One text only discussed pronoun contractions, without suggesting instructional procedures or activities. Another text did mention Richek's research (36) regarding potential sources of difficulty in comprehension of pronouns (see Chapter 5) but omitted instructional procedures and activities. Two texts briefly provided instructional ideas but failed to discuss research.

In my opinion, the ideal college text contains the following elements regarding the comprehension of anaphoric structures:

1. A detailed listing and description of the various types of anaphoric structures;

2. A discussion of the textual, language, and experiential variables affecting comprehension of anaphoric structures;

3. An explanation of how the teacher can help readers comprehend anaphoric structures with direct instruction and modeling;

4. A description of a wide variety of activities for instruction and reinforcement in comprehension of anaphoric structures.

Since no text included all of these elements, it is apparent that anaphoric resolution needs to receive increased attention from teacher trainers.

Table 2
Professional Texts' Coverage of Pronouns

	Description of Structures	Experimental Theoretical Discussion	Instructional Ideas
Aukerman and Aukerman (2)	X		
Aulls (3)	X		X
Cunningham, Cunningham, and Arthur (12)			X
Harris and Sipay (21)		X	
Karlin (26)			X
Pearson and Johnson (33)	X	X	X
Zintz (40)			X

Summary

Research indicates that the use of various types of anaphoric structures may affect reading comprehension and that some children are better at comprehending those structures than are others. An informal survey of current instruction in anaphoric reference in basal series and college methods textbooks revealed considerable variation in the attention given to this skill in basal series and that remarkably few college texts prepare teachers in this area. Activities that are used in basal series have also been presented.

References

1. Aaron, I.E., D. Jackson, C. Riggs, R.G. Smith, and R.J. Tierney. *Scott, Foresman Reading.* Glenview, IL: Scott, Foresman, 1981.

2. Aukerman, R.C., and L.R. Aukerman. *How Do I Teach Reading?* New York: John Wiley and Sons, 1981.

3. Aulls, M. *Developing Readers in Today's Elementary Schools.* Boston: Allyn and Bacon, 1982.

4. Barnitz, J.G. "Developing Sentence Comprehension in Reading," *Language Arts,* 1979, *56* (8), 902-908, 958.

5. Barnitz, J.G. "Syntactic Effects on the Reading Comprehension of Pronoun-Referent Structures by Children in Grades Two, Four, and Six," *Reading Research Quarterly,* 1980, *15* (2), 268-289.

6. Bormuth, J.R., J. Manning, J. Carr, and P.D. Pearson. "Children's Comprehension of Between- and Within-Sentence Syntactic Structures," *Journal of Educational Psychology,* 1970, *61,* 349-357.

7. Chai, D.T. *Communication of Pronominal Referents in Ambiguous English Sentences for Children and Adults.* Ann Arbor: University of Michigan, 1967. (ED 012 889)

8. Chapman, L.J. "The Comprehension of Anaphora," paper presented at the the twenty-sixth annual convention of the International Reading Association, New Orleans, 1981.

9. Chapman, L.J. "The Importance of the Notion of Cohesion for Teachers of Reading," paper presented at the eighteenth annual conference of the United Kingdom Reading Association, 1981.

10. Clark, H.H., and C.J. Sengul. "In Search of Referents for Nouns and Pronouns," *Memory and Cognition,* 1979, *7* (1), 35-41.

11. Clymer, T., D. Gates, and C.M. McCullough. *Ginn Reading 360 Program.* Lexington, MA: Ginn, 1973.

12. Cunningham, J.W., P.W. Cunningham, and S.V. Arthur. *Middle and Secondary School Reading.* New York: Longman, 1981.

13. Durkin, D. *Reading Comprehension Instruction in Five Basal Reader Series* (Reading Educ. Rep. No. 26). Urbana, IL: Center for the Study of Reading, University of Illinois, 1981.

14. Durkin, D. *What is the Value of the New Interest in Reading Comprehension?* (Reading Educ. Rep. No. 19). Urbana, IL: Center for the Study of Reading, University of Illinois, 1980.

15. Dutka, J.T. "Anaphoric Relations, Comprehension and Readability," in P.A. Kolers, M.E. Wrolstad, and H. Bouma (Eds.), *Processing of Visible Language 2.* New York: Plenum Press, 1980.

16. Early, M., E.K. Cooper, N. Santeusanio, and M. Adell. *The Bookmark Reading Program,* second edition. New York: Harcourt Brace Jovanovich, 1974.

17. Evertts, E., L. Hunt, and B. Weiss. *The Holt Basic Reading System.* New York: Holt, Rinehart and Winston, 1973.
18. Fay, L., R.R. Ross, and M. LaPray. *Rand McNally Reading Program: Young America Basic Series.* Chicago: Rand McNally, 1978.
19. Garvey, C., A. Caramazza, and J. Yates. "Factors Influencing Assignment of Pronoun Antecedents," *Cognition,* 1976, *3,* 227-243.
20. Gottsdanker-Willekens, A.E. "The Interference of Some Anaphoric Expressions on Reading Comprehension," *Reading Psychology,* 1981, *2* (3), 132-145.
21. Harris, A.J., and E.R. Sipay. *How to Increase Reading Ability,* seventh edition. New York: Longman, 1980.
22. Irwin, J.W. "The Effect of Linguistic Cohesion on Prose Comprehension," *Journal of Reading Behavior,* 1980, *12* (4), 325-332.
23. Johnson, I.M., A.R. Ramirez, M.B. Smith, J.C. Manning, J.M. Wepman, L.M. Sullivan, W.A. Jenkins, I.E. Aaron, H.M. Robinson, A.S. Artley, and M. Monroe. *The New Open Highways.* Glenview, IL: Scott, Foresman, 1974.
24. Johnson, M.S., R.A. Kress, and J.D. McNeil. *American Book Reading Program.* New York: American Book Company, 1977.
25. Kameenui, E.J., and D.W. Carnine. "An Investigation of Fourth Graders' Comprehension of Pronoun Constructions in Ecologically Valid Texts," *Reading Research Quarterly,* 1982, *17,* 556-580.
26. Karlin, R. *Teaching Elementary Reading: Principles and Strategies,* second edition. New York: Harcourt Brace Jovanovich, 1975.
27. Lesgold, A.M. "Variability in Children's Comprehension of Syntactic Structures," *Journal of Educational Psychology,* 1974, *66,* 333-338.
28. Moberly, P.C. "Elementary Children's Comprehension of Anaphoric Relationships in Connected Discourse," unpublished manuscript, University of Washington, 1981.
29. Moberly, P.C., and D.L. Monson. "Effect of Instruction on Fifth Graders' Comprehension of Anaphoric Structures," unpublished manuscript, University of Washington (undated).
30. Monson, D. "Effect of Type and Direction on Comprehension of Anaphoric Relationships," paper presented at the International Reading Association/Word Research conference, 1982.
31. O'Donnell, M. *Harper and Row Design for Reading.* New York: Harper and Row, 1972.
32. Otto, W., M. Rudolph, R. Smith, and R. Wilson. *The Merrill Linguistic Reading Program.* Columbus, OH: Charles E. Merrill, 1975.
33. Pearson, P.D., and D.D. Johnson. *Teaching Reading Comprehension.* New York: Holt, Rinehart and Winston, 1978.
34. *Pronoun Pinch Hitter.* Allen, TX: Developmental Learning Materials, 1978.
35. Richek, M.A. "The Effects of Paraphrase Alternation and Sentence Complexity on Wh-Questions," paper presented at the American Educational Research Association annual meeting, 1975.
36. Richek, M.A. "Reading Comprehension of Anaphoric Forms in Varying Linguistic Contexts," *Reading Research Quarterly,* 1976/1977 (2), 145-165.
37. Teddlie, J. "Discourse Effects on Children's Resolution and Recall of Anaphoric Relationships," doctoral dissertation, Texas Woman's University, 1979.
38. Webber, B.L. *A Formal Approach to Discourse Anaphora.* New York: Garland Press, 1978.
39. Webber, B.L. "Syntax Beyond the Sentence: Anaphora," in R.J. Spiro, B.C. Bruce, and W.F. Brewer (Eds.), *Theoretical Issues in Reading Comprehension.* Hillsdale, NJ: Erlbaum, 1980.
40. Zintz, M.V. *The Reading Process: The Teacher and the Learner,* third edition. Dubuque, IA: Wm. C. Brown, 1980.

James F. Baumann
Jennifer A. Stevenson

9

Teaching Students to Comprehend Anaphoric Relations

In Chapter 2 we presented a "Selective Taxonomy of Anaphoric Relations"—a taxonomy, we argued, that lends itself to instructional applications as well as to research. In Chapter 5 the literature related to readers'
abilities to comprehend anaphoric relationships was reviewed, and from
this review it is apparent that young and developing readers have considerable difficulty resolving anaphora in connected text—that is, making the
proper anaphoric-term/antecedent association. In this chapter we address
the issue of effectively *teaching* children to comprehend anaphoric relations. The emphasis on teaching is important, since our concern here is to
provide teachers guidance in how to instruct children to comprehend
anaphora, rather than to provide methods for testing or researching anaphoric relations.

We have organized this chapter into three sections. In the first part, we
present a strategy suitable for teaching anaphora, which draws on teacher
effectiveness research and recent comprehension instructional research. In
the second section, we present two model lessons that employ this teaching
strategy. One lesson involves an anaphora skill appropriate for primary
level (second grade) students; the second lesson is intended for upper ele-
mentary/middle school (sixth grade) students. In the third part, we present
practice exercises and games teachers can use to reinforce previously
taught anaphora skills.

An Instructional Strategy for Teaching Anaphora

During the past decade much has been learned about the underlying cognitive and psychological processes involved in reading comprehension (*21, 26, 31*), but only recently have researchers addressed the issue of how to *teach* reading comprehension skills effectively (*16, 19, 30, 34*). Although there is not a large body of extant comprehension instructional research, results of the few studies that have been conducted are encouraging. Drawing from the vast store of research on teacher effectiveness (e.g., *2, 6, 7, 8, 10, 14, 15, 27, 28*), comprehension instructional studies employing the principles of direct instruction (*6, 11*) have demonstrated that children can be taught specific comprehension skills. For example, Hansen (*17*) and Hansen and Pearson (*18*) effectively taught children to increase their inferential comprehension skill; Raphael and Pearson (*25*) reported positive effects of metacognitive training on children's question-answering strategies; and Tharp (*33*) reported consistently higher levels of reading comprehension in a longitudinal study involving educationally high risk, Polynesian-Hawaiian primary grade children who received massed, active comprehension instruction when compared to children in a more traditional decoding-focused program. As Pearson (*20*) concluded after reviewing these and other studies (see additional reviews *22, 23, 24*), "The data are encouraging. It looks as though we can teach comprehension skills after all" (p. 22).

What are the characteristics of effective comprehension instruction? Teacher effectiveness research and successful comprehension instruction research (see synthesis reviews in *2, 6, 8, 9, 20, 22, 23, 24, 28*) indicate that children learn reading comprehension skills when: 1) adequate time is devoted to comprehension instruction, 2) students attend to instruction and are engaged in meaningful activities, 3) teachers provide significant amounts of direct instruction in specific comprehension skills, 4) students are provided feedback about their success in skill acquisition, 5) teachers provide application and transfer tasks, and 6) massed practice follows instruction.

The strategy we present here (adapted from references *1* and *5*) incorporates these elements of effective instruction and is suitable for teaching children to comprehend anaphoric relations. The strategy consists of four steps: 1) Introduction/Example, 2) Direct Instruction, 3) Teacher-Directed Application, and 4) Independent Practice. Another important aspect of the strategy is that the responsibility for the performance of the anaphora skill gradually shifts from full teacher responsibility (Introduction/Example and Direct Instruction) to shared teacher/student responsibility (Teacher-Directed Application) to full student responsibility (Independent Practice) (see *1, 23, 24*). This shift of responsibility helps students internalize the anaphora skill and promotes transfer and independent application of the skill during subsequent independent reading. A description of each of the four steps follows.

Baumann and Stevenson

Introduction/Example

When teachers have clearly formulated instructional objectives, and when they are able to communicate them effectively to children, learning is enhanced (7, 29, 35). In the Introduction/Example step, the teacher tells students what skill will be taught and why the acquisition of this skill will make them better readers. With this introduction, the teacher provides an example of the target skill. This Introduction/Example will take only a few minutes, but it is important because it provides the students with a structured overview of the lesson that will follow. Thus, students are left with a clear statement of the content and purpose of the ensuing lesson and have seen an example of the anaphora skill under consideration.

Direct Instruction

Research confirms the commonsense notion that students learn what they have been taught (6, 7, 10, 14). In other words, formal, direct instruction is the most efficient manner to communicate information and transmit skills. This step, therefore, is the real heart of the anaphora instructional strategy. Although Duffy and Roehler (11) point out that the term *direct instruction* has many different definitions and interpretations, for the purpose of the anaphora instructional strategy, we offer the following definition: *Direct instruction* occurs when the teacher, in a face-to-face, reasonably formal manner, tells, shows, models, demonstrates, teaches the skill to be learned. The critical word in the definition is *teacher,* for it is the teacher who is in command of the learning situation; the teacher leads the lesson, as opposed to having a worksheet, kit, learning center, or workbook constitute instruction. In this step, as was true of the Introduction/Example step, the teacher still assumes full responsibility for learning. Students are not passive, but the teacher is in charge, leading the lesson and teaching the anaphora skill.

Teacher-Directed Application

In order for skills acquired during direct instruction to transfer to non-instructional settings, direct instruction must be followed by application exercises and feedback to students about their success in skill acquisition (9, 11). In the Teacher-Directed Application step, the teacher provides students with guided application of the skill that was previously taught, using materials not used in instruction. In addition, feedback to students (and to the teacher) occurs, so monitoring of skill acquisition is possible. In this step in the anaphora instructional strategy, the teacher and the pupil share responsibility for learning (1, 23, 24). The teacher still initiates the activities, but the students are required to puzzle out texts that contain the anaphora skills previously taught. In other words, the teacher is still present for guidance and feedback, but the students are weaned from teacher support. What differentiates this from simple practice (as in the final step, Independent Practice) is that the teacher still directs the lesson, and the teacher and students *together* work through application exercises. This permits the teacher to evaluate informally how well students have learned the skill, so that reteaching can occur if necessary. The students are also provided with immediate feedback about their performance, so that they can be reassured that they are applying the skill properly, or can receive corrective instruction. To promote transfer, increasingly larger units of text can be used in the application step.

Independent Practice

Any model of learning requires massed practice of the skills that have been taught (9, 20). Although practice alone does not ensure learning, the learner ultimately must be able to apply a reading skill independently in novel situations without teacher assistance. In the Independent Practice step, the transition from full teacher responsibility to shared pupil/teacher responsibility to full pupil responsibility is completed. The student now must exercise the skill independently in comprehending the anaphora element previously taught and applied. To promote transfer further, students practice the anaphora skill within the context of reading exercises using unaltered, natural passages (e.g., selections from basal readers or trade books).

It should be noted that the preceding instructional strategy has been shown to be effective in two research studies. In one study, Baumann (3) randomly assigned sixth grade students to one of three treatments: a direct instruction group which was taught a series of main idea skills according to the four step instructional strategy; a basal group which received massed instruction on main idea from a basal reader series; or a control group which received vocabulary development instruction. Results revealed that the direct instruction group significantly outperformed both the basal and control groups on a series of measures that assessed varying aspects of main idea comprehension. In a second, similar study, Baumann (4) used the instructional strategy to teach third grade students to comprehend anaphoric relationships. Using the Selective Taxonomy of Anaphoric Relationships presented in Chapter 2, this group was taught noun, verbal, and clausal substitute anaphoric term/antecedent associations. On a series of posttests, the group using the four part instructional strategy outperformed both a basal and control group, again indicating that systematic, intensive instruction of reading comprehension skills is effective and efficient in achieving the desired outcome of skill acquisition. Therefore, there is some empirical support for the value of using this instructional approach for teaching main idea and anaphora skills.

Model Lessons

In this section we present two model lessons for teaching the comprehension of specific anaphoric relations. Each model lesson employs the

Baumann and Stevenson

four step instructional strategy outlined in the preceding section. The first lesson, designed for second graders, involves the comprehension of simple personal pronouns (Anaphora Type I-A-1 from the Selective Taxonomy presented in Chapter 2). The second model lesson, intended for sixth graders, teaches students how to comprehend inclusive verb and clausal substitutes (Anaphora Type II-A and Type III-A from the Selective Taxonomy). Lessons involving other anaphora elements from the Selective Taxonomy would follow the format of these two model lessons; in other words, while the content would differ and the complexity of the anaphora and the difficulty of the exercises would need to be adjusted for the reading ability of the students, instructional techniques would be similar for all lessons.

The two model lessons that follow are preceded by a lesson objective and a description of the students for whom the lesson is intended. Each lesson is then organized according to the four step instructional strategy. For convenience, statements the teacher makes directly to students are presented in uppercase type; other comments and annotations are printed in lowercase type; linguistic examples are in italics.

Anaphora Model Lesson One

  Objective: Teach students to comprehend simple personal pronoun anaphora; specifically, students will be able to associate a previously stated antecedent with a subsequent anaphoric term (personal pronoun, singular or plural; e.g., *girl/she* or *girls/they*).

  Level: Second grade

  Group: Small or large group instruction of students reading at the second grade level (i.e., students reading in a 2^1 or 2^2 level basal reader). For students above or below this level, the lesson should be modified so that the application and independent practice exercises are at an appropriate difficulty level.

Introduction/Example: WHEN PEOPLE WRITE, THEY SOMETIMES USE WORDS THAT STAND FOR OTHER WORDS. FOR EXAMPLE, LOOK AT THE TWO SENTENCES I HAVE WRITTEN ON THE BOARD:
   Mark is my best friend. He lives next door.
CAN ANYONE READ THESE TWO SENTENCES? Student response. GOOD. IN THE FIRST SENTENCE FIND THE WORD *Mark*. Student response. IN THE SECOND SENTENCE FIND THE WORD *he*. Student response. *He* AND *Mark* ARE THE SAME PERSON. *He* STANDS FOR THE WORD *Mark*. *He* MEANS *Mark*. I AM GOING TO READ THE SENTENCES FOR YOU, BUT THIS TIME I'M GOING TO USE THE WORD *Mark* IN BOTH SENTENCES. Teacher reads the sentences substituting *Mark* for *he* in the second sentence. NOTICE THAT WHETHER I SAY *he* OR *Mark* IN THE SECOND SENTENCE, THE SENTENCE STILL MEANS

THE SAME THING. THIS IS AN EXAMPLE OF WHAT WE WILL LEARN ABOUT TODAY: HOW ONE WORD CAN STAND FOR ANOTHER WORD. THIS IS AN IMPORTANT READING SKILL BECAUSE WRITERS OFTEN USE TWO DIFFERENT WORDS TO MEAN THE SAME THING. IF YOU DON'T KNOW WHAT WORDS GO TOGETHER, YOU CAN GET MIXED UP WHEN YOU READ. BUT IF YOU CAN FIGURE OUT WHAT WORDS GO TOGETHER, THAT WILL HELP YOU UNDERSTAND WHAT YOU ARE READING. WHEN WE FINISH OUR LESSON TODAY, YOU SHOULD BE ABLE TO FIGURE OUT WHAT SOME WORDS SUCH AS *he, she, it, we, you* AND *they* STAND FOR. (Note: It may be best not to provide the label *pronoun* for students at this point, since this is unnecessary for the successful acquisition of this particular anaphora skill and may detract from the focus of the lesson.)

Direct Instruction. NOW LOOK AT THE PAIRS OF SENTENCES I HAVE WRITTEN ON THE BOARD.

1. Mother baked a cake. <u>It</u> was good.
2. Jane left for school early. <u>She</u> was feeling ill.
3. Today is John's birthday. Sally gave <u>him</u> a toy truck.
4. Dick and John are twins. <u>They</u> are ten years old today.
5. "Come to the store with me," said Mary. "No," said Terry, "<u>You</u> go by yourself."

CAN ANYONE READ THE SENTENCES AFTER NUMBER 1? Student response. GOOD. NOW TRY TO ANSWER THIS QUESTION: WHAT WAS GOOD? Student response (*cake*). RIGHT! WHAT WORDS STANDS FOR *cake* IN THE SECOND SENTENCE? WHAT WORD IS USED INSTEAD OF THE WORD *cake?* Student response (*it*). YES, THE WORD *it* STANDS FOR *cake* IN THE SECOND SENTENCE.

CAN ANYONE GO UP TO THE BOARD AND DRAW AN ARROW FROM *it* TO *cake?* Selected student completes task. GOOD. NOW, CAN ANYONE GO UP TO THE BOARD AND WRITE THE WORD THAT *it* STANDS FOR ABOVE THE WORD *it?* Student completes task. CORRECT. THE WORD *cake* STANDS FOR *it.* NOW LET'S READ THESE SENTENCES TOGETHER BUT SAY THE WORD *cake* FOR *it* IN THE SECOND SENTENCE. Teacher and students read the sentences in unison.

NOTICE THAT IN ALL THESE PAIRS OF SENTENCES, THERE IS AN UNDERLINED WORD IN THE SECOND SENTENCE. THAT WORD STANDS FOR ANOTHER WORD IN THE SENTENCE THAT COMES BEFORE IT. NOW LOOK AT THE SENTENCES AFTER NUMBER 2. LISTEN WHILE I READ THEM ALOUD. Teacher reads sentence aloud. WHO WAS FEELING ILL? Student response (*Jane*). THAT'S CORRECT. WHAT WORD IN THE SECOND SENTENCE STANDS FOR THE WORD *Jane*? Student response (*she*). HOW DID YOU KNOW THAT JANE WAS ILL? Student response. RIGHT, JANE IS A GIRL AND THE WORD *she* TELLS YOU THAT A GIRL IS BEING TALKED ABOUT. CAN SOMEONE GO UP TO THE BOARD AND DRAW AN ARROW FROM *she* TO THE WORD THAT *she* STANDS FOR? Student completes task. CAN SOMEONE WRITE THE WORD THAT *she*

Baumann and Stevenson

STANDS FOR ABOVE THE WORD *she?* Student completes task. GOOD. NOW LET'S READ BOTH SENTENCES TOGETHER BUT LET'S SAY THE WORD *Jane* FOR THE WORD *she* IN THE SECOND SENTENCE. Teacher and students read the sentences in unison.

Sentences 3, 4, and 5 would be completed in a similar manner. The teacher can stop when convinced that the students have acquired the concept of anaphoric-term/antecedent association and then move on to the next portion of Direct Instruction.

NOW LOOK AT THE STORY I HAVE WRITTEN ON THE BOARD.

1. Kathy, Tom, and Sally are friends.
2. When they were walking home from school one day, Kathy said,
3. "Why don't we make a club?"
4. Kathy added, "We could call it Oak Street Club,
5. since we all live on Oak Street."
6. That's a good idea," said Tom.
7. Sally said, "Yes, I think we should make a club."
8. "All right," said Kathy, but you have to help decide who will be president."
9. "Yes," said Tom, "We need to have an election."
10. They agreed with him and decided to have an election the next day.

IN THIS STORY YOU SEE SOME WORDS THAT ARE UNDERLINED. ALL OF THE UNDERLINED WORDS STAND FOR OTHER WORDS, JUST LIKE THEY DID IN THE SENTENCES WE LOOKED AT BEFORE. LISTEN WHILE I READ THE STORY ALOUD, AND THEN WE'LL TRY TO FIGURE OUT WHAT WORD OR WORDS EACH OF THE UNDERLINED WORDS STANDS FOR. Teacher reads the story orally, pausing briefly at each anaphoric term.

NOW LET'S GO THROUGH THE STORY SENTENCE BY SENTENCE AND SEE IF WE CAN FIGURE OUT WHAT WORDS THE UNDERLINED WORDS STAND FOR. Teacher reads lines 1, 2, and 3. IN LINE 2, I READ THE WORD *they.* WHO ARE *they?* WHAT WORD OR WORDS DOES *they* STAND FOR? Student response (*Kathy, Tom,* and *Sally*). YES, *they* STANDS FOR *Kathy, Tom,* and *Sally*. LOOK AT LINE 3. WHAT WORD OR WORDS DOES *we* STAND FOR? WHO ARE *we?* Student response (*Kathy, Tom,* and *Sally*). CORRECT! AGAIN, *we* STANDS FOR *Kathy, Tom,* AND *Sally*. CAN SOMEONE COME UP TO THE BOARD AND WRITE THE WORDS *they* AND *we* STAND FOR RIGHT ABOVE THEM? Selected student completes task.

Proceeding in a similar manner for the entire story, the teacher should also point out how the same anaphoric term may have different referents; for example, *they* in line 2 refers to all three children, whereas *they* in line 10 refers only to *Kathy* and *Sally*. A good concluding exercise would be to read through the story inserting all the antecedents for the anaphoric terms.

Teacher-Directed Application. HERE IS A WORK PAPER WE ARE GOING TO DO TOGETHER. Teacher distributes "Group Exercise: Words that Stand for Other Words."

Figure 1. Teacher-directed application exercise for model lesson one (second grade).

Name _____

Words that stand for other words

A. 1. (Rachel) worked outside all morning. She cut the grass and swept the sidewalk.

2. Chris and Pat are good friends. They play together every day.

3. Mark said, "Cindy, why don't you be the team captain?"

4. Mr. and Mrs. Jones want to buy a new car. They decided it should be red.

5. Mary closed the door, and then she locked it.

6. Tom's dog is Max. He feeds him dog food every day after supper.

7. The three boys built a tree fort. When they were done, they decided it needed a coat of green paint.

Skunk, Fox and Wolf

B. Skunk, Fox, and Wolf are good friends. They live in an old hollow tree.

One day, Skunk said, "I think we should move and find a new home."

"I agree with you," said Fox. "This old tree is cold and dirty."

"Wait a minute," said Wolf. "I like this old tree. It has been my home

for five years. You can go and find a new home, but I am going to live here."

LOOK AT PART A. HERE ARE SOME SENTENCES. IN THESE SENTENCES YOU WILL FIND SOME UNDERLINED WORDS. WHAT I WANT YOU TO DO IS TO TRY TO FIGURE OUT WHAT WORD OR WORDS STAND FOR EACH UNDERLINED WORD. THEN CIRCLE THE WORDS THAT GO WITH EACH UNDERLINED WORD. FINALLY, DRAW AN ARROW FROM THE UNDERLINED WORD TO THE WORD(S) YOU CIRCLED. NUMBER 1 HAS BEEN DONE FOR YOU. Teacher reads number 1 to make sure the students understand the task. NOW TRY TO DO THE REST OF PART A ON YOUR OWN. Teacher allows sufficient time to complete Part A.

OK, LET'S SEE HOW WELL YOU DID. CAN ANYONE READ NUMBER 2? Student response. WHAT WORD OR WORDS DID YOU CIRCLE IN NUMBER 2? Student response *(Chris and Pat)*. THAT'S CORRECT, THE WORD *they* STANDS FOR *Chris and Pat*. HOW ABOUT NUMBER 3? The teacher would proceed through the application exercises asking various students to respond. If one or more students are having difficulty, reteaching can occur at this point.

NOW LOOK AT PART B. PART B IS A WHOLE STORY. WHAT YOU MUST DO HERE IS READ THE STORY AND FIGURE OUT WHAT WORD OR WORDS THE UNDERLINED WORDS STAND FOR. BUT IN THIS STORY, ALL YOU NEED TO DO IS WRITE THE WORDS IN THE BLANK ABOVE EACH UNDERLINED WORD. THE FIRST ONE HAS BEEN DONE FOR YOU. The teacher reads the first two sentences and explains that *they* stands for *Skunk, Fox,* and *Wolf.* NOW TRY TO COMPLETE THE REST OF PART B ON YOUR OWN.

The teacher would again allow time for the students to complete the exercise independently. Upon completion, a guided discussion of the correct answers would occur. This provides the teacher with feedback about the students' skill acquisition and the students with feedback about their success in mastering this skill. If the students have difficulty completing this exercise, the teacher would provide additional examples and reteach the anaphora skill.

Note: Many different Teacher-Directed Application exercises are possible. In fact, many of the activities included in the following portion of this chapter ("Activities to Practice and Reinforce Anaphora Comprehension") would be appropriate here if used in an application manner.

Independent Practice. THE LAST THING I HAVE FOR YOU IS A WORK PAPER FOR YOU TO COMPLETE AT YOUR DESKS. Teacher distributes "Independent Practice: Words that Stand for Other Words."

Figure 2. Independent practice exercise for model lesson one (second grade).

Name _____

INDEPENDENT PRACTICE
Words that stand for other words

Directions: Read the following story and try to figure out what each underlined word stands for. Then write the word or words that each underlined word stands for in the blank above it. The first one has been done for you.

"Nobody Listens to Andrew"*
by Elizabeth Guilfoile

Andrew
Andrew saw something upstairs. He ran down very fast. He said, "Listen, Mom."

Mom said, "Wait, Andrew. I must take Grandma to the bus. She must get the bus before dark."

"Listen, Dad," Andrew said. "I saw something upstairs."

Dad said, "Wait, Andrew. I must cut the grass before dark."

"Nobody listens to me," thought Andrew.

Andrew said, "Listen, Ruthy. I saw something upstairs. It was in my bed."

Ruthy said, "I can't stop now, Andrew. I must find my bat and ball. I want to play ball before dark."

"Nobody listens to me," thought Andrew.

Andrew saw Mr. Pond walking his dog. Andrew said, "Mr. Pond, I saw

――――   ――――

something upstairs. It was in my bed. It was black."

Mr. Pond said, "I can't listen to you now, Andrew. I must take my dog for
a walk before dark."

Andrew shouted, "Listen Mom. Listen, Dad. Listen, Ruthy. Listen, Mr. Pond. Listen,
Grandma. THERE IS A BEAR UPSTAIRS IN MY BED!"

Mom stopped. She said, "Call the police."

Dad stopped. He said, "Call the fire house."

Ruthy stopped. She said, "Call the zoo."

Mr. Pond stopped. He called the police. He called the fire house. He called the zoo.

Zoom! came the police.
Zoom! came the fire truck.
Zoom! came the woman from the zoo.

They all ran upstairs. "Look!" said Mom. "It is black."

"Look!" said Dad. "It is in the bed."

"Look!" said Ruthy. "It's a bear! Andrew said it was a bear but nobody listens to Andrew."

The police said, "It must have come from the woods. It climbed up the tree.

It climbed in the window."

The woman from the zoo said, "It is dry in the woods. The bears are looking for water.

I will take this bear to the zoo."

Everyone looked at Andrew. They all said, "Next time we will listen to Andrew."

*From *Nobody Listens to Andrew* by Elizabeth Guilfoile, copyright © 1957 by Modern
Curriculum Press, Inc. Used by permission of Modern Curriculum Press, Inc.

REMEMBER LAST WEEK WHEN WE READ THE STORY "NOBODY LISTENS
TO ANDREW"? THIS STORY IS PRINTED ON THIS WORK PAPER, AND IN THE
STORY YOU WILL FIND MANY UNDERLINED WORDS. WHAT I WANT YOU TO
DO IS TO TRY TO FIGURE OUT WHAT EACH OF THESE UNDERLINED WORDS
STANDS FOR, AND THEN WRITE YOUR ANSWERS IN THE BLANKS ABOVE THE
UNDERLINED WORDS. THE FIRST ONE HAS BEEN DONE FOR YOU. The teacher
works through these examples with the children until they understand how
to complete the exercise. NOW GO BACK TO YOUR DESKS AND COMPLETE
THE WORK PAPER. REMEMBER, WHAT YOU HAVE TO DO IS TO TRY TO FIGURE

OUT WHAT WORD OR WORDS MEAN THE SAME AS THE UNDERLINED WORD.
TAKE YOUR TIME AND WORK CAREFULLY.

Note: "Nobody Listens to Andrew" is from a 2^1 level basal reader. This material was selected for independent practice because it is natural text (original prose not designed specifically for skill instruction) and provides practice of the anaphora skill within a passage-length selection. As in the Teacher Directed step, however, many different practice exercises are possible. The following section of this chapter provides additional examples of practice exercises.

Anaphora Model Lesson Two

Objective:	Teach students to comprehend inclusive verb substitute anaphora; specifically, students will be able to associate a previously stated antecedent with a subsequent anaphoric term (pro-verb or pro-clause, see Selective Taxonomy in Chapter 2). (Note that both Type II-A and Type III-A anaphora are included in one lesson because they go together logically and because the distinction between them is often confusing and arbitrary.)
Level:	Sixth grade
Group:	Small or large group instruction of students reading at or near the sixth grade level (i.e., students reading in a fifth or sixth grade level basal reader). For students above or below this level, the lesson should be modified so that the application and independent practice exercises are at an appropriate difficulty level.
Assumption:	Students will have had prior instruction in noun substitute anaphora (Type I from the Selective Taxonomy); hence, they will be familiar with the concept of anaphora, although unfamiliar with pro-verbs (words substituted for preceding verbs) and pro-clauses (words substituted for preceding clauses).

Introduction/Example. REMEMBER OUR LESSONS LAST WEEK WHEN WE LOOKED AT HOW WRITERS USE CERTAIN WORDS TO STAND FOR OTHER WORDS? Student response. IN THOSE LESSONS WE LEARNED HOW SIMPLE PERSONAL PRONOUNS ARE USED TO STAND FOR OTHER WORDS. WE THEN LEARNED HOW DEMONSTRATIVE PRONOUNS (LIKE *this* AND *that*) ARE ALSO USED TO STAND FOR OTHER WORDS. AND FINALLY, WE LEARNED HOW GENERAL TERMS AND WORDS THAT STAND FOR SEVERAL THINGS (LIKE *some, both, many*) ALSO REFER BACK TO OTHER WORDS.

TODAY WE WILL CONTINUE TO LOOK AT WORDS THAT STAND FOR OTHER WORDS, BUT NOW WE WILL CONSIDER WORDS THAT ARE USED TO REPLACE VERBS AND ENTIRE CLAUSES. REMEMBER THAT A VERB IS A WORD THAT TELLS ABOUT ACTION OR BEING. EXAMPLES OF VERBS ARE WORDS

LIKE *run, am,* OR *happen.* VERBS, LIKE NOUNS, CAN ALSO BE REPLACED BY OTHER WORDS. LOOK AT THE FOLLOWING EXAMPLE:

Tommy likes pizza. Sarah does too.

IN THE FIRST SENTENCE, WE LEARN THAT TOMMY LIKES PIZZA. THE SECOND SENTENCE DOESN'T DIRECTLY SAY THAT SARAH LIKES PIZZA, BUT WE KNOW THAT SHE DOES BECAUSE THE WORDS *does too* TELL US SO. THEREFORE THE WORDS *does too* STAND FOR THE WORDS *likes pizza.* TO PROVE THIS, CAN SOMEONE READ BOTH SENTENCES BUT SUBSTITUTE THE WORDS *likes pizza* FOR THE WORDS *does too* IN THE SECOND SENTENCE? Student response. GOOD. NOTICE THAT THE SECOND SENTENCE STILL MEANS THE SAME THING WHETHER YOU SAY *likes pizza* OR *does too.*

THIS IS WHAT WE WILL LEARN ABOUT TODAY — HOW DIFFERENT WORDS CAN BE USED IN PLACE OF VERBS AND CLAUSES. THIS IS AN IMPORTANT READING SKILL BECAUSE WRITERS OFTEN SUBSTITUTE WORDS FOR VERBS, AND IF YOU DON'T KNOW WHAT WORDS GO TOGETHER — WHAT WORDS MEAN THE SAME — YOU MAY GET CONFUSED WHEN YOU READ. THEN YOU WON'T COMPREHEND VERY WELL. BUT IF YOU CAN FIGURE OUT WHAT WORDS STAND FOR, OR REFER TO, A CERTAIN VERB, YOU WILL UNDERSTAND BETTER WHAT YOU ARE READING. (Note that the distinction between a simple pro-verb and a more complex pro-clause is never explicitly made in this lesson. This distinction is not made because it is probably not necessary to be consciously aware of this distinction in order to resolve these anaphora and because the explanation might confuse the students unnecessarily.)

Direction Instruction. LOOK AT THE SETS OF SENTENCES I HAVE WRITTEN ON THE BOARD:

1. Harry ate three green apples. Martha did too.
2. Tim can catch a ball very well. So can Matt.
3. Mark was angry, and he told his teacher so.
4. Carl has been bowling well lately, and so have I.

CAN ANYONE READ THE SENTENCE AFTER NUMBER 1? Student response. GOOD. DID HARRY EAT THREE GREEN APPLES? Student response *(yes).* HOW CAN YOU TELL? Student response. YES, IT SAYS SO EXACTLY IN THE FIRST SENTENCE. DID MARTHA EAT ANY GREEN APPLES? Student response *(yes).* ALL RIGHT, I AGREE, BUT HOW CAN YOU TELL? IT DOESN'T SAY EXACTLY THAT MARTHA ATE THREE GREEN APPLES. Student response. WHAT WORDS IN THE SECOND SENTENCE TOLD YOU THAT SHE ALSO ATE GREEN APPLES? Student response *(did too).* YES, IN THE SECOND SENTENCE, THE WORDS *did too* WERE USED IN PLACE OF THE WORDS *ate three green apples.* IN OTHER WORDS, THE VERB *ate* AND THE OBJECT OF THE VERB *three green apples* WERE REPLACED BY THE WORDS *did too.*

COULD I HAVE A VOLUNTEER? Student response. SAM, GO UP TO THE BOARD AND DRAW A CIRCLE AROUND *ate three green apples.* NOW DRAW A CIRCLE AROUND THE WORDS *did too.* AND FINALLY, DRAW AN ARROW FROM *did too* TO *ate three green apples.* Student response. THIS ARROW SHOWS

Baumann and Stevenson

THE RELATIONSHIP BETWEEN THESE TWO SETS OF WORDS—HOW *did too* STANDS FOR, REPLACES, OR REFERS TO, THE WORDS *ate three green apples.* The teacher proceeds in a similar manner with the other examples until students understand simple pro-verbs and pro-clauses in single and adjacent sentences.

NOW LOOK AT THE SHORT STORY I HAVE WRITTEN ON THE BOARD:

1. Jack and Jane went to Henry's Hamburger House for lunch.
2. Jack ordered a hamburger, but Jane <u>didn't</u>. Instead, she
3. ordered a fish sandwich. Jane ordered french fries and
4. Jack <u>did too</u>, but Jane ordered a root beer and Jack <u>didn't.</u>
5. He said he would rather order a chocolate shake. And he <u>did.</u>
6. Jane said, "I like my lunch," and Jack responded, "I <u>do too.</u>"

IN THIS STORY YOU FIND SOME UNDERLINED WORDS. ALL THESE WORDS STAND FOR OTHER PARTS OF THE STORY. LISTEN WHILE I READ THE STORY ALOUD AND SEE IF YOU CAN DETERMINE WHAT VERBS THESE UNDERLINED WORDS STAND FOR. Teacher reads story.

ALL RIGHT, LET'S LOOK AT THE FIRST PART OF THE STORY. IN LINE 2 IT SAYS THAT JACK ORDERED A HAMBURGER BUT JANE DIDN'T. NOW, THE WORD *didn't* REFERS BACK TO PART OF THAT SENTENCE. WHO CAN TELL US WHAT PART *didn't* STANDS FOR? Student response. CORRECT. IT REFERS TO *ordered a hamburger,* ALTHOUGH HERE IT MEANS JANE DID NOT ORDER A HAMBURGER. NOW, WHO CAN CIRCLE THE PART OF THE SENTENCE THAT *didn't* REFERS TO AND THEN DRAW AN ARROW FROM *didn't* TO THE WORDS YOU CIRCLE? Student response. GOOD. Again, the teacher works through the story pointing out the anaphoric relations or having the students discover them. The critical part of direct instruction is to have the students make the coreferential link between anaphoric term and antecedent, for the potential barrier to comprehension involves students' inability to associate the antecedent with the appropriate anaphoric term.

Teacher-Directed Application. I AM HANDING OUT A WORK PAPER WE WILL COMPLETE TOGETHER. Teacher distributes "Group Exercise: Words that Substitute for Verbs and Clauses."

LOOK AT PART A, NUMBER I. READ THE SENTENCE TO YOURSELF AND SEE IF YOU CAN FIGURE OUT WHAT THE WORDS *does too* STAND FOR. WHEN YOU DECIDE WHAT THEY REFER TO, WRITE THOSE WORDS IN THE BLANK AT THE END OF THE SENTENCE. Students complete the exercise. OK, WHO CAN TELL ME WHAT THE WORDS *does too* STAND FOR? Student response. CORRECT, *does too* STANDS FOR *like to ride bikes,* SO WHEN IT SAYS *Jessica does too,* IT MEANS THAT JESSICA LIKES TO RIDE BIKES ALSO. NOW COMPLETE NUMBERS, 2, 3, AND 4 ON YOUR OWN. Students complete exercises, and the teacher then reviews their responses, reteaching or clarifying errors if necessary.

NOW LOOK AT PART B ON YOUR PAPER. IN THIS SECTION YOU MUST ANSWER QUESTIONS ABOUT SOME SENTENCES. GO AHEAD AND READ THE SENTENCES, AND THEN WRITE THE ANSWERS YOU THINK ARE CORRECT.

Figure 3. Teacher-directed application exercise for model lesson two (sixth grade).

Name _____

Words that substitute for verbs and clauses

A. 1. I like to ride bikes, and Jessica does too. _____

    2. The elephant is large, as is the rhinoceros. _____

    3. Homer will join the Boy Scouts. So will José. _____

    4. Is it true you are moving away? Ron says so. _____

B. 1. Max enjoys math class, but Monica doesn't.

    Who likes math? _____ Who dislikes math? _____

    2. Sandra is a good reader, as is Tommie.

    Who reads well? _____ How are Sandra and Tommie alike? _____

    3. Candy said, "You better sign up for soccer, Randy, for I already have."

    "No," replied Randy, "You might enjoy soccer, but I don't."

    Who has signed up for soccer? _____

    Who likes soccer? _____ Who dislikes soccer? _____

C. 1. Connie and Kim were walking home from school together.

    2. "You know, Kim," said Connie, "I think Dennis Johnson is a creep."

    3. "Me too," said Kim. "He never leaves anyone alone."

    4. "Yes," replied Connie. "He always calls me names."

    5. "And Ralph Otto too," said Kim. "But at least Tommy Barnet doesn't."

    6. "Yes," said Connie, "He's a nice boy."

Students complete exercise. ALL RIGHT, LET'S SEE HOW WELL YOU DID. NUMBER I SAYS "MAX ENJOYS MATH CLASS, BUT MONICA DOESN'T." HOW DID YOU ANSWER THE QUESTION, "WHO LIKES MATH?" Student response. YES, IT SAYS DIRECTLY THAT MAX ENJOYS MATH. WHAT ABOUT THE SECOND QUESTION, "WHO DISLIKES MATH?" Student response (Monica dislikes math). DOES ANYONE ELSE AGREE? Student response. WELL, HOW CAN YOU

TELL THAT MONICA DISLIKES MATH? IT DOESN'T SAY SO IN THOSE SENTEN-
CES. Student response. Teacher completes the remaining exercises clarifying and reteaching if necessary.

IN THE FINAL SECTION OF THIS PAPER, PART C, YOU WILL FIND A SHORT
STORY. NOTICE THAT THERE ARE THREE UNDERLINED PARTS OF THE STORY.
READ THROUGH THE STORY AND TRY TO FIGURE OUT WHAT OTHER PARTS
OF THE STORY THESE UNDERLINED SECTIONS REFER TO. Teacher allows
time for students to read story and find antecedents for identified anaphora. OK, WHAT ABOUT THE WORDS *me too* IN LINE 3? Teacher reviews the
exercise giving the students feedback on their work and simultaneously
evaluating how well they have mastered pro-verbs and pro-clauses.

Independent Practice. THE LAST THING I HAVE FOR YOU TO DO IS A
WORK PAPER YOU CAN COMPLETE DURING YOUR STUDY PERIOD. Teacher
distributes "Independent Practice: Words that Stand for Other Words."

Figure 4. Independent practice exercise for model lesson two (sixth grade).

Name _____

INDEPENDENT PRACTICE
Words that stand for other words

Directions. Read the following story and try to figure out what each underlined part stands
for. Then write the word or words each underlined part stands for in the numbered blanks at
the end of the story.

from "Tales of Myrtle the Turtle"*
by Keith Robertson

My brother Witherspoon can ask some of the silliest questions for a turtle, especially a
turtle from such an intelligent family as ours. Yesterday, right out of a blue sky, he (1) asked
Aunt Myrtle why turtles had never invented an automobile.

"That's (2) very simple," Aunt Myrtle said scornfully, "No turtle ever wanted a car."

"I do (3)," Witherspoon said. "I'd like a nice little sports car; bright red would be about
right."

"I beg your pardon," Aunt Myrtle said. "What I should have said is that no turtle in his
right mind ever wanted a car."

"I do (4)," said Witherspoon. "But I think I've changed my mind. I would like a bright
blue one (5)."

"My statement still stands," Aunt Myrtle said. "There are various reasons humans invent
such things as cars and turtles do not (6)."

"Such as (7)?" Witherspoon said.

"It is unbearably hot today," Aunt Myrtle said. "I need a rest. When I wake up from my
short nap, we will resume this argument, silly though it (8) is."

She closed her eyes and a minute later was snoring softly. Witherspoon crept up quietly and looked closely at Aunt Myrtle. Then he came over and whispered in my ear. "Nap, my eye. She's (9) pretending to sleep while she thinks up some answer for me!"

"She's not (10) either!" I said. "Aunt Myrtle is probably the wisest turtle in the world, except possibly for Uncle Herman. I've never met him (11)."

1. _____

2. _____

3. _____

4. _____

5. _____

6. _____

7. _____

8. _____

9. _____

10. _____

11. _____

From *Tales of Myrtle the Turtle* by Keith Robertson. Copyright © 1964 by Keith Robertson. Reprinted by permission of Viking Penguin Inc.

ON THIS WORK PAPER YOU SEE PART OF THE STORY FROM "TALES OF MYRTLE THE TURTLE" WHICH WE READ A FEW WEEKS AGO. IN THIS STORY YOU WILL FIND I I DIFFERENT UNDERLINED PARTS, ONE OR TWO WORDS EACH. WHAT I WANT YOU TO DO IS TO READ THROUGH THIS STORY CARE-FULLY AND TRY TO DETERMINE WHAT THESE UNDERLINED WORDS STAND FOR. SOME OF THEM WILL BE SIMPLE PRONOUNS THAT STAND FOR NAMES OF PERSONS OR THINGS. SOME, HOWEVER, WILL STAND FOR VERBS OR LARGER PARTS OF SENTENCES. WRITE THE WORDS FROM THE STORY THAT THE UN-DERLINED PARTS STAND FOR IN THE BLANKS AT THE END OF THE STORY. DOES ANYONE HAVE A QUESTION? Teacher responds to questions and makes sure students understand the task. TAKE YOUR TIME AND WORK CAREFULLY, BECAUSE SOME OF THESE WILL BE RATHER DIFFICULT.

Note: This independent practice exercise, like the one accompanying Model Lesson One, is taken directly from a basal reader (grade 6 in this case). Obviously, other practice exercises are also possible. Additional examples of practice and reinforcement activities are contained in the following section.

Baumann and Stevenson

Activities to Practice and Reinforce Anaphora Comprehension

The following activities are designed to provide reinforcement and practice of anaphora skills which have been taught previously. All of the activities are adaptable to a variety of grade levels if the readability of the examples and the complexity of the anaphora are appropriate for the level of the students. Activities are classified into three categories: 1) traditional paper and pencil activities; 2) activities involving flash cards and other manipulatives; and 3) game and puzzle exercises.

Paper and Pencil Activities

The following activities are similar to exercises commonly found in basal reader series. The basal activities, however, usually reinforce only pronoun-antecedent relationships and do not include other anaphora. The exercises below use standard formats but also include other anaphoric relationships. Before a teacher assigns independent practice exercises like these, students must understand the tasks they are required to do. To insure this, teachers should present many examples before students complete the exercises independently.

Find the Antecedent. This activity requires students to locate and identify antecedents for anaphoric terms. For young children, use simple sentences and sentence pairs; for older students, paragraphs or passage length selections may be used. The following examples present several different formats for matching anaphoric terms to their antecedents.

1. *Directions:* Circle the word or words that mean the same as the underlined word or words. The first one has been done for you.
   (a) (Sam) went fishing all morning. He caught two bass and a perch.
   (b) My bike is very old. For my birthday I'm going to get a new one.
   (c) Mary scored two goals in last night's soccer game. Mary's teammate, Susan, did too.
   (d) Terry and Tom went swimming. Both had a great time.
   (e) The Brownies went to visit the fire station, but several couldn't go because they had the flu.

2. *Directions:* The following story has several underlined words. Try to figure out what other word or words mean the same as the underlined words. Write your answers on the spaces below. The first one has been done for you.

My name is Tom. I[1] have a best friend whose name is Jim. We[2] have a lot in common. I[3] like to ride bikes, and so does[4] Jim. Jim likes to play soccer, and so do[5] I[6]. Like I[7] said, my friend[8] and I enjoy doing the same things.

1. _____Tom_____   5. _____

2. _____   6. _____

3. _____   7. _____

4. _____   8. _____

Note: This activity can be made less difficult by giving students a list of answer choices.

3. *Directions:* Below are two stories that give the same information. The story on the left has some words underlined in it. Look in the story on the right and find a word or words that mean the same as each underlined part. Then circle these words and put the number by the part you circled. The first one has been done for you.

Kathy and Connie went to Mc-Donald's for lunch. When they¹ got there,² they both³ ordered a cheeseburger. Kathy ordered a regular fry, and so did⁴ Connie. When⁵ the girls⁶ finished, they⁷ hopped on their bikes and rode home.

Kathy and Connie went to Mc-Donald's for lunch. When (Kathy and Connie) got to McDonald's, Kathy and Connie ordered cheeseburgers. Kathy ordered a regular fry, and Connie ordered a regular fry. When Kathy and Connie were through eating, Kathy and Connie hopped on their bikes and rode home.

Anaphora Substitution. In this activity the student substitutes an anaphoric term for a clearly identified antecedent. The following activities are similar to the "Find the Antecedent" exercises, the difference being that students need to select an abbreviated, more efficient way of stating repeated information.

1. *Directions:* Each of the following sentences contains one or more underlined words. From the list at the bottom of the page, select a

word that means the same as the underlined part and write that word on the blank. The first one has been done for you.

(a) <u>John</u> went on a trip to New York.

(a)   *He*

(b) Mary built a doghouse. She made <u>the doghouse</u> for her pet poodle.

(b) _____

(c) Nancy went to Bear Lake Camp last summer. She had never been <u>to Bear Lake Camp</u> before.

(c) _____

(d) Mark hit a home run, and Tom <u>hit a home run.</u>

(d) _____

(e) Martha got some new building blocks for her birthday, but her brother came along and broke the <u>new building blocks.</u>

(e) _____

them   did too   he   there   it

2. *Directions:* The following story has some underlined parts. Read the story and try to think of another way you could say what the underlined parts mean. Write your answers on the blanks above the underlined parts. The first one has been done for you.

                           1. <u>They</u>   2. _____
John and Mary went to the zoo. <u>John and Mary</u> rode the bus <u>to the zoo.</u>
                  3. _____   4. _____
When <u>John and Mary</u> arrived <u>at the zoo</u>, they decided to go to the monkey

house. The monkeys were very frisky and hungry. John and Mary bought
                5. _____   6. _____
some peanuts for <u>the monkeys</u> and fed <u>the peanuts</u> to the monkeys. Next
7. _____
<u>John and Mary</u> decided to go and see the elephants. The elephants were

eating hay, and John and Mary were surprised to see the
8. _____   9. _____
<u>great amount of hay</u> the elephants could eat. <u>The elephants eating hay</u>
       10. _____
made <u>John and Mary</u> hungry, so John bought a hot dog and Mary

11. _____ 12. _____
bought a hot dog. After John and Mary ate their hot dogs, they walked
                              13. _____
over to see the lions and tigers. After they saw the lions and tigers,
14. _____   15. _____
John and Mary visited the camel pen and buffalo cage. John and Mary
                    16. _____
decided to go home, and John and Mary rode the bus all the way
17. _____
home.

Question/Answer Activities. Requiring students to respond to questions about anaphoric relationships will help them make these associations and ultimately improve reading comprehension. The following activities are designed for this purpose, but they can also be used for evaluating students' ability to comprehend anaphora.

1. *Directions:* Read the sentences below and then answer the questions that follow.

   (a) Carla painted a pretty picture,   What does it refer to?
       and then she gave it to
       her mother.   _____

   (b) These sweet rolls are stale.   What does ones refer to?
       Can't you get some fresh ones?   _____

   (c) You better sign up for   What does have refer to?
       ballet, for I already have.   _____

2. *Directions:* Read the sentences and short paragraphs below, and then write answers to the questions that follow.

   (a) John had a birthday. Because of this, Sally gave him a new watch.

       Who received the gift? _____
       Why was the gift given? _____

   (b) Martin and Monica made an attractive couple. The woman wore a long black coat, and the man's coat was white with tails.

       Whose coat was white? _____
       Whose coat was black? _____

   (c) John is thrifty, but Mary isn't. The boy always saves his allowance, but the girl always spends her money on gum and candy.

       Is Mary thrifty? _____
       Who would have more money? _____
       Who do you think would be better at blowing bubbles? _____

(d) Ronald owns an antique bicycle. He got it from his grandfather who used it when he was a child. At that time, the bicycle was considered to be very "fancy."

From whom did Ronald get the bicycle? _____

Who first owned the bicycle? _____

When was the bicycle considered to be "fancy"? _____

(e) The Boy Scouts scheduled an activity day last Saturday. The scouts could choose what they wanted to do. Some learned how to tie knots. Most of the scouts went to the movie on bear hunting. Only a few decided to learn sign language. At the end of the day, everyone got together for cookies and hot chocolate.

How many scouts ate cookies and hot chocolate? _____

Did many scouts choose to learn how to tie knots? _____

What was the most popular activity? _____

What was the least popular activity? _____

3. *Directions:* Read the story below and then answer the questions that follow.

(1) Tom, John, and Barry are the best of friends. They all live
(2) on Mulberry Street and attend Woodlawn Elementary School.
(3) Tom is a third grader, but the other two are in the next grade.
(4) Tom was the first to join the Boys' Club, but John and Barry
(5) were quick to follow. Barry likes football and marbles, and
(6) so do the others. Tom collects stamps, and so do the others.
(7) You might say that each of them is a pea in the same pod.

(a) In what grade is John? _____

(b) In line (3), what does the other two refer to? _____

(c) In line (6), what does so do the others mean? _____

(d) In line (5), what does were quick to follow mean? _____

Other Paper-and-Pencil Activities. Several other less structured exercises can help children understand the relationship between anaphoric terms and their antecedents.

1. Discuss specific kinds of anaphora (e.g., personal pronouns, demonstrative pronouns, arithmetic) and have students list all the anaphoric terms under discussion from a short passage. Then have them write the antecedent word or words for each anaphoric term.

2. As an extension of the preceding activity, have students rewrite the original story substituting antecedents for all anaphoric terms. This will demonstrate how useful anaphora are in decreasing the redundancy of word usage in written and oral language.

3. Have students select a common anaphoric term (e.g., *he, she, they*) and then examine a story to identify this anaphoric term each time it appears. Then have the students list the antecedent for the word each time it appears. Next, examine these lists and point out that any given anaphoric term might have several different antecedents, and that proper comprehension is dependent upon using the context of the story to make the correct associations.

Flash Cards and Other Manipulatives

The following activities involve children physically in learning how to comprehend anaphoric relationships. The exercises include using flash cards in a variety of ways, and also other manipulative devices.

Flash cards. Flash cards requiring anaphoric term/antecedent associations can be simply made by writing on one side of a card a sentence or two in which an anaphoric term is underlined. On the reverse side, write the antecedent (answer). Figure 5 shows two examples of this type of flash

Figure 5. Sample "Find the Antecedent" anaphora flash cards.

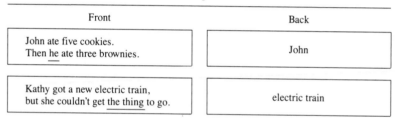

Front	Back
John ate five cookies. Then <u>he</u> ate three brownies.	John
Kathy got a new electric train, but she couldn't get <u>the thing</u> to go.	electric train

Figure 6 gives examples of flash cards in which students must substitute an anaphoric term for an antecedent.

Figure 6. Sample "Anaphora Substitution" flash cards.

Front	Back
<u>Donald and Zelda</u> went to the movies.	they
Sue drew a picture, and <u>Jenny drew a picture</u>.	did too

Flash card activities.

1. It is appropriate for students, either individually or in pairs, to work with sets of flash cards that contain anaphora of suitable difficulty. In addition, any small group flash card games commonly

used with sight words or math facts will work well with anaphora flash cards.

2. Many commercial or teacher-made "track" games adapt well for use with anaphora flash cards. When the student is required to "pick a card," s/he must select an anaphora card and successfully make the appropriate association in order to move the marker.

3. "Anaphora Concentration" can be played with special sets of anaphora flash cards. Sets of cards (of either the antecedent matching or anaphora substitution variety) can be constructed so that one set contains the phrase or sentence and the other set contains the "answers." Students can then take turns selecting one card from each set, retaining all correct matches. The student with the greatest number of correct matches wins.

4. Many other traditional classroom flash card games can be conducted using anaphora flash cards. Games such as "Around the World" and "Baseball" will adapt well for use with cards that require students to make anaphoric associations.

Other manipulatives.

1. A "computer" can be constructed from a milk carton, so that a student can insert an anaphora flash card in the input slot, seeing only one side of the card. After first guessing the appropriate answer, the student inserts the card into the computer and it emerges from the output slot with the reverse side (answer) showing. (See Figure 7.)

Figure 7. Anaphora computer.

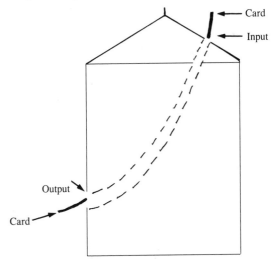

2. Anaphora Dominoes can be constructed by writing short sentences on one half of a paper or cardboard domino, and then underlining a word or words (within the sentences) for which an anaphoric term can be substituted. On the other half of the domino, print antecedents which match other anaphoric terms. Then, traditional dominoes can be played. See the example in Figure 8 in which the anaphoric term *she* has been matched with the antecedent *Mary*.

Figure 8. Anaphora dominoes.

Their	Mary has a cat.	She	Tom and Sue are friends.

Games and Puzzles

A variety of games and puzzles can require children to make anaphoric associations. Several examples are listed below, but an imaginative teacher will also be able to develop many additional activities.

1. Anaphora Bingo cards can be constructed by writing anaphoric terms in the boxes. In this game the Caller selects flash cards that contain short phrases in which an antecedent is identified. The players must then think of possible anaphoric terms that will substitute for the antecedent and cover the corresponding words on their

Figure 9. Anaphora bingo.

BINGO				
HE	THEN	IT	DID TOO	HER
THAT	ITS	THEM	YOU	BOTH
THEM	WE	**FREE**	OUR	HERE
I	MY	ALL	YOUR	NONE
SOME	MINE	SHE	HE	SHE

cards. For example, the Caller might say: "Tom and Mary played tag. Find a word that will mean the same as Tom and Mary." Ideally, the flash cards will be large enough to place on the chalk tray so all the players can see them well. Figure 9 presents a sample bingo card.

2. A variation of Anaphora Bingo is Pronoun Whirl, a game designed for young students who need work on pronoun antecedents. Make a spinner that contains common pronouns and a game board with boxes containing short sentences with underlined antecedents. Two or three students can play. Students alternately spin the arrow and then see if they can find a sentence in which the pronoun can be substituted. They may then put a colored marker (different colors for each player) on that square. When all the squares are filled, the student with the most markers on the board is the winner. A sample spinner and a portion of a game board are shown in Figure 10.

Figure 10. Pronoun whirl spinner and game board.

Mary and I are eight years old.	You go with Tom's grandfather.
Tommie has a new goldfish.	Dad painted the house green.
Both of the boys have 5¢.	Tom, Jim, and Mark ate pizza.
Ride with Mom and Dad.	Mary has five blue marbles.

3. Anaphora Design lends itself nicely to a learning center situation. The teacher constructs worksheets that contain geometric designs. Within each shape, a sentence with a blank space is written. Sentences are designed so that only certain anaphoric terms will "fit." A key in which these anaphoric terms are matched with colors is also made. The student must determine which anaphora fit, and then color each shape the appropriate color. Figure 11 gives an example.

Figure 11. Sample anaphora design.

she = red   *this* = yellow   *so does* = green   *us* = blue

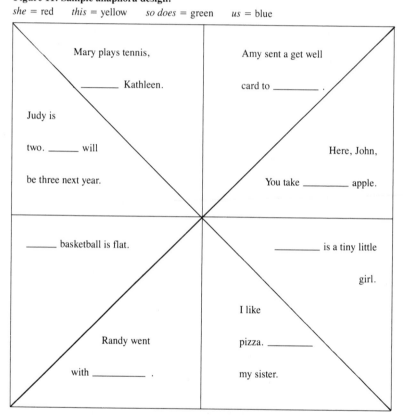

4. Anaphora crossword puzzles can also be constructed substituting antecedents for all anaphoric terms in a passage. Students must read the passage and supply a substitute word or words for the antecedents and then fill in the crossword puzzle with these words. Young children may need a list of answer words. See Figure 12.

Figure 12. Sample anaphora crossword puzzle.

1 across

John and his cousin went to the fair last week. John and his cousin had a great time

7 across   2 across

at the fair. First, John and his cousin took a ride on the roller coaster.

    3 down   6 down

The roller coaster was really fast. John got sick. John's cousin got sick also.

                     8 across

Then they went to see the gorilla. What a crazy gorilla. First, it threw peanuts at the crowd.

    4 across

Then the gorilla pounded its chest. After that they went on six more rides, but they liked only

    1 down   2 down

three of the rides. Finally they went home and they were glad to be home.

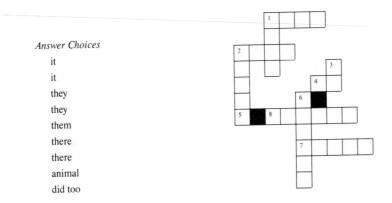

Answer Choices

it

it

they

they

them

there

there

animal

did too

Summary and Conclusions

In this chapter we have presented a strategy for teaching children to comprehend anaphoric relationships. The strategy is based on recent research and theory explaining the principles of effective comprehension instruction. Two sample lessons demonstrate the application of this strategy to teaching specific anaphora skills. Finally, we have included many practice and reinforcement exercises and games which teachers can use to provide students with practice with the anaphora skills that have been taught.

We have prepared such a detailed discussion of anaphora comprehension instruction because evaluations of existing reading instructional materials, primarily basal readers, have revealed that little instruction in anaphora comprehension exists in these materials (*12, 13, 32;* Chapter 8). We are not so naive, however, as to expect every classroom teacher to create an entirely original series of lessons for teaching anaphora. Teachers seldom have the luxury of expending the time and effort required to develop such a set of lessons. Rather, what we hope is that teachers will: 1) become aware of the *need* for formal, direct instruction in anaphora comprehension; 2) use our Selective Taxonomy of Anaphoric Relationships (Chapter 2) as a content outline for anaphora instruction; 3) adapt or extend the lessons in commercial materials; and 4) when necessary, develop anaphora comprehension lessons which begin with existing materials and then incorporate the instructional features presented in this chapter.

References

1. Baumann, J.F. "A Generic Comprehension Instructional Strategy," *Reading World,* 1983, *22,* 284-294.
2. Baumann, J.F. "Implications for Reading Instruction from the Research on Teacher and School Effectiveness," *Journal of Reading,* 1984, *28,* 109-115.
3. Baumann, J.F. "The Effectiveness of a Direct Instruction Paradigm for Teaching Main Idea Comprehension," *Reading Research Quarterly,* 1984, *20,* 93-115.
4. Baumann, J.F. "Teaching Third Grade Students to Comprehend Anaphoric Relationships: The Application of a Direct Instruction Model," *Reading Research Quarterly,* in press.
5. Baumann, J.F., and J.A. Stevenson. "How to Really Teach Reading Comprehension," paper presented at the Twenty-Seventh Annual Convention of the International Reading Association, Chicago, April 1982.
6. Berliner, D.C. "Academic Learning Time and Reading Achievement," in J.T. Guthrie (Ed.), *Comprehension and Teaching: Research Reviews.* Newark, DE: International Reading Association, 1981.
7. Berliner, D.C., and B.V. Rosenshine. "The Acquisition of Knowledge in the Classroom," in R.C. Anderson, R.J. Spiro, and W.E. Montague (Eds.), *Schooling and the Acquisition of Knowledge.* Hillsdale, NJ: Erlbaum, 1977.
8. Brophy, J., and T.L. Good. "Teacher Behavior and Student Achievement," in M.C. Wittrock (Ed.), *Third Handbook of Research on Teaching.* New York: Macmillan, in press.
9. Brown, A.L., J.C. Campione, and J.D. Day. "Learning to Learn: On Training Students to Learn from Texts," *Educational Researcher,* 1981, *10,* 14-24.
10. Duffy, G.G. "Teacher Effectiveness Research: Implications for the Reading Profession," in M.L. Kamil (Ed.), *Directions in Reading: Research and Instruction,* Thirtieth Yearbook of the National Reading Conference. Washington, D.C.: National Reading Conference, 1981.
11. Duffy, G.G., and L.F. Roehler. "Direct Instruction of Comprehension: What Does It Really Mean?" *Reading Horizons,* 1982, *23*(1), 35-40.
12. Durkin, D.D. "Reading Comprehension Instruction in Five Basal Reader Series," *Reading Research Quarterly,* 1981, *16,* 515-544.
13. Durkin, D.D. "What Is the Value of the New Interest in Reading Comprehension?" *Language Arts,* 1981, *58*(1), 23-43.
14. Fisher, C.W., D.C. Berliner, N.N. Filby, R.S. Marliave, L.S. Cahen, and M.M. Dishaw. "Teaching Behaviors, Academic Learning Time, and Student Achievement: An Over-

view," in C. Denham and A. Liberman (Eds.), *Time to Learn*. Washington, DC: National Institute of Education, 1980.

15. Good, T., and J. Brophy. *Looking in Classrooms*. New York: Harper and Row, 1984.
16. Guthrie, J.T. (Ed.). *Comprehension and Teaching: Research Reviews*. Newark, DE: International Reading Association, 1981.
17. Hansen, J. "The Effects of Inference Training and Practice on Young Children's Reading Comprehension," *Reading Research Quarterly*, 1981, *16*, 391-417.
18. Hanse, J., and P.D. Pearson. "An Instructional Study: Improving the Inferential Comprehension of Good and Poor Fourth Grade Readers," *Journal of Educational Psychology*, 1983, *79*, 821-829.
19. Langer, J.A., and M.T. Smith-Burke (Eds.). *Reader Meets Author/Bridging the Gap: A Psycholinguistic and Sociolinguistic Perspective*. Newark, DE: International Reading Association, 1982.
20. Pearson, P.D. *A Context for Instructional Research on Reading Comprehension* (Technical Report No. 230). Champaign, IL: Center for the Study of Reading, University of Illinois, 1982.
21. Pearson, P.D. (Ed.). *Handbook of Reading Research*. New York: Longman, 1984.
22. Pearson, P.D. "Direct Explicit Teaching of Comprehension," in G.G. Duffy, L.R. Roehler, and J. Mason (Eds.), *Comprehension Instruction: Perspectives and Suggestions*. New York: Longman, 1984.
23. Pearson, P.D. "Changing the Face of Reading Comprehension Instruction," *Reading Teacher*, 1985, *38*, 724-738.
24. Pearson, P.D., and M.C. Gallagher. "The Instruction of Reading Comprehension," *Contemporary Educational Psychology*, 1983, *8*, 317-344.
25. Raphael, T., and P.D. Pearson. *The Effect of Metacognitive Training on Children's Question-Answering Behavior* (Technical Report No. 238). Champaign, IL: Center for the Study of Reading, University of Illinois, 1982.
26. Reder, L.M. *Comprehension and Retention of Prose: A Literature Review* (Technical Report No. 108). Champaign, IL: Center for the Study of Reading, University of Illinois, 1978.
27. Rosenshine, B.V., and D.C. Berliner. "Academic Engaged Time," *British Journal of Teacher Education*, 1978, *4*, 3-16.
28. Rosenshine, B.V., and R. Stevens. "Classroom Instruction in Reading," in P.D. Pearson (Ed.), *Handbook of Reading Research*. New York: Longman, 1984.
29. Samuels, S.J. "Characteristics of Exemplary Reading Programs," in J.T. Guthrie (Ed.), *Comprehension and Teaching: Research Reviews*. Newark, DE: International Reading Association, 1981.
30. Santa, C.M., and B.L. Hayes (Eds.). *Children's Prose Comprehension: Research and Practice*. Newark, DE: International Reading Association, 1981.
31. Spiro, R.J., B.C. Bruce, and W.F. Brewer (Eds.). *Theoretical Issues in Reading Comprehension: Perspectives from Cognitive Psychology, Linguistics, Artificial Intelligence, and Education*. Hillsdale, NJ: Erlbaum, 1980.
32. Stevenson, J.A., and J.F. Baumann. "Helping Children Comprehend Anaphoric Relationships (Pronouns, Pro-Verbs, Deleted Nouns): Definition, Research, and Instructional Suggestions," paper presented at the Twenty-Sixth Annual Convention of the International Reading Association, New Orleans, April 1981.
33. Tharp, R.G. "The Effective Instruction of Comprehension: Results and Description of the Kamehameha Early Education Program," *Reading Research Quarterly*, 1982, *17*, 503-527.
34. Tierney, R.J., and J.W. Cunningham. "Research on Teaching Reading Comprehension," in P.D. Pearson (Ed.), *Handbook of Reading Research*. New York: Longman, 1984.
35. Tikunoff, W., D.C. Berliner, and R.C. Rist. *An Ethnographic Study of the Forty Classrooms of the Beginning Teacher Evaluation Study Known Sample* (Technical Report No. 75-10-5). San Francisco: Far West Regional Laboratory for Educational Research and Development, 1975.

10

Charles H. Clark

Instructional Strategies to Promote Comprehension of Normal and Noncohesive Text

The degree to which a text is cohesive affects the degree to which it seems to be a unified whole as opposed to a seemingly random collection of unrelated sentences. Readers are confronted with the task of producing a sufficiently cohesive memory representation to permit comprehension and retention. In many cases, cohesion inferences are needed to provide missing linking information. The success of this task depends on the reader's ability to apply rather sophisticated strategies. These strategies are susceptible to instruction; in other words, they can be taught.

This chapter presents several instructional techniques designed to improve reading comprehension and inferencing ability. These techniques can be adapted to teach students how to comprehend noncohesive texts.

Because so much of the current teacher practice is based on direct questioning, a section will deal with ways to improve such questioning. Even with modification of teacher questioning strategies, though, questioning alone is not sufficient to improve comprehension. No matter how effective the questioning, direct postreading questioning is still primarily product related and must be combined with effective process oriented teaching techniques, so teaching of comprehension monitoring, ReQuest, and the Guided Reading Procedure will also be discussed.

Comprehension Monitoring

Successful comprehension of text which lacks explicit cohesion requires skill in two particular areas: The reader must first recognize a tex-

125

tual violation which disrupts comprehension, and then apply a strategy to overcome the difficulty. The first step in resolving any comprehension problem is, of course, recognizing that a problem exists. Beginning readers, in particular, may not always be aware of their own comprehension processes and may not realize when even simple difficulties arise. In the following sentences, for instance, a beginning or nonproficient reader may make a simple referent assignment without recognizing the inherent ambiguity.

> Jane asked Alice to go to the corner store with her. She bought a candy bar for her sister and one for herself. Alice's mother was angry at her for spending money on candy.

Though the referent for "She" in the second sentence is unclear, most readers would assign it to Jane. If later evidence contradicts the original and most probable assignment in the third sentence, the nonproficient reader is likely to maintain the incorrect assignment. Although, as will be discussed later, tentative referent assignments are a practical and productive strategy for dealing with ambiguous pronouns, the less skilled reader may treat the initial assignment of the referent as permanent and so may not re-evaluate the referent assignment despite the conflicting information in the later sentence. This conflict would not be subject to resolution, but would instead further disturb the understanding of the text. The proficient reader, on the other hand, would be more likely to be aware that the initial assignment of the anaphoric reference was tentative and to revise that assignment if the later text conflicted with it.

In addition to recognizing comprehension problems caused by cohesion breaks, the proficient reader has well developed strategies for solving such problems. Proficient readers typically solve such problems in one of the following ways, organized in order of implementation, difficulty, and the degree to which the remedy disrupts reading (1). These strategies are normally learned during the process of becoming a proficient reader. They are rarely taught, though they can be taught in a systematic manner as will be discussed later.

Hierarchy of Comprehension Problem Solving Strategies

1. Ignoring the portion of the text in question and continuing to read is the first, easiest, and least disruptive solution, particularly effective with relatively minor problems not crucial to the text. If the ignored information turns out to be important, the ignored text can be reread. It is particularly advantageous for students to learn that they can repeal any comprehension judgment (such as that to ignore a section of text)—one can always retreat and reread the material.

2. Suspending judgment on the immediate text portion is a logical extension of the first strategy. However, instead of totally ignoring the con-

tent, the reader continues reading in hopes that later text will clarify the difficulty. This is frequently viable since authors often clarify and develop issues after their initial introduction.

3. Successful readers may form tentative hypotheses in the face of ambiguity. This trial comprehension or memorial representation depends heavily upon both the reader's background knowledge and his/her understanding of the text. (The previewing technique discussed later in this chapter is ideal for facilitating background knowledge use.) Typically, the more knowledgeable the reader is in the subject area and the better the reader's general skills, the more likely that the hypothesis formulated will be sufficiently correct. Both the ReQuest and Guided Reading Procedure instructional techniques discussed later in this chapter are particularly helpful in teaching students to develop and monitor such interpretations.

4. Rereading the current or prior text is rather more disruptive than the previous strategies (though it is an integral part of those strategies, particularly when they fail), but it provides an opportunity to reinterpret the text. This is particularly helpful when ambiguities or contradictions are not resolvable any other way.

5. Going to an expert source, or leaving the text for help, is the most disruptive technique used by proficient readers (and the least frequent). However, especially in cases where the text is making no sense whatsoever, it may be the only alternative.

The following paragraph will be used to illustrate these processes and strategies:

> John's father asked him to go to the hardware store to buy a box of nails. On his way there (1) he saw his friend Sam. He (2) was on his way home from a little league baseball game. He (3) liked to build things with his hands. John asked Sam to go the store with him. They walked around the store talking about the expensive tools. As they were leaving John noticed a bulge in Sam's jacket. The jacket was tight. (4) The zipper slipped down. Out came the nails, right in front of the owner. He (5) was arrested for stealing. John's father was very angry when they (7) called him.

With the exception of 4 and 6, which mark implicit connectives, all of the above numbers indicate anaphoric references. Pronoun number 3 above could be successfully ignored since the remainder of the text in no way refers to the information in that sentence, i.e., no information makes an incorrect referent assignment apparent or important. A good reader, then, might either make no assignment at this point or assign the pronoun to either referent without encountering any conflict later in the text. The reader can suspend judgment with number 2 since the remainder of that sentence clarifies the referent—John was on his way to the store, not on his way home from a baseball game, so "Sam" must be the correct referent. The proficient reader encountering item number 1 would probably make a tentative referent assignment to the hardware store, and later text would support this. Item number 4 indicates the position of an implied connective (that the zipper slipped because the jacket was tight and something was making it bulge). The proficient reader will hypothesize this missing causal connective, and later information would not contradict this guess. The last three items are interrelated. The most logical hypothesis for item 5 is the referent "Sam," since Sam had the bulge in his jacket. However, upon finishing the first part of the next sentence, indicating that it was John's father who was upset, the reader may want to revise the hypothesis and use "John" as the referent for 5. Item 6 also requires a causal inference that John's father was angry because he (John or Sam) had been arrested. The last pronoun, number 7, can refer to either John or Sam, to John or Sam with the police, or to the police themselves without either main character. At this point, the ending of the tale is sufficiently confusing that even a good reader would have difficulty. Such difficulty can be solved by formation of a hypothesis or, because of the severity of the problem, the reader may choose to ask the teacher or another reader to clarify the ambiguity.

Teaching the Monitoring Process through Modeling

The instructional goals for modeling instruction include making the students constantly aware of their comprehension and any comprehension difficulties and helping them learn to deal with these problems (1). The students should, therefore, be able to recognize and deal with implicit cohesion relations (connectives) by appropriately inferring cohesion relations and they should be able to designate an ambiguous anaphoric reference appropriately. Modeling instruction is ideal for cohesion instruction since students who do not deal with cohesion problems often lack specific strategies rather than ability. Modeling, as described below, emphasizes such process oriented learning (see 1).

In stage one of instruction, the teacher reads aloud and simultaneously makes comments about the reading. The teacher should pause once or twice per paragraph to comment on his/her comprehension processes. In teaching cohesion inferencing, the teacher should, for instance, generate any hypotheses that come to mind concerning cohesion relations. If a hypothesis turns out to be incorrect, the teacher should say so, explain why it now seems incorrect, and model and discuss the process of hypothesis revision. Students will need to observe not only the process and reasoning behind the initial development of a hypothesis, but also the process behind its evaluation and revision. Using the paragraph about John and Sam above, the teacher would probably pause at each marked place. The teacher monologue might, for instance, proceed as follows:

> "On his way there," I wonder where "there" is? It must be the hardware store since that was the only place mentioned.

When the teacher reads the section containing items 5-7, things start to get interesting. At first, the teacher will probably assign "Sam" as the referent to "he" (#5).

> "John's father was very angry." Now why was John's father angry? Sam was the one who tried to steal the nails. He should have been the one who was arrested. The police didn't arrest both of them, since the last sentence said that "He was arrested." John's father could have been angry because John was with Sam when he did the stealing and John was supposed to buy the nails with money he had given John. I'll read some more and we'll find out if I am right. "John's father was very angry when they called him." "They" must mean the police. But why did the police call him? They should have called Sam's father. Let's continue the reading and see if there is anything later which clears this up....

In general, the teacher should verbally monitor his/her comprehension, continuously asking questions which a proficient reader must answer to maximize comprehension. While resolving those issues, the teacher should explain the issues involved in solving cohesion problems, including the five strategies typically used by proficient readers (ignoring the text, suspending judgment, hypothesis formation, rereading, and using an outside resource). The teacher should make different referent assignments on a trial basis, discussing the effects on the meaning of the text for each, and testing all logical connective inferences. If something in the text is difficult to understand, the teacher should indicate this to the students and explain why the text is unclear. Honest doubt about a particular interpretation should be expressed when an average reader would experience such doubt. The teacher should avoid always being right the first time.

After the students become familiar with this stage in the training, the teacher should encourage an increase in the level of student participation in the verbalized comprehension process. This participation should naturally increase with encouragement from the teacher. The students can propose tentative cohesive ties, volunteer reasons and justifications for particular interpretations and referent assignments, and suggest strategies for dealing with particular problems.

Once the students are participating, the second stage of the procedure has been initiated: the student participation stage. During this stage, the students should develop, evaluate, and revise their hypotheses, as the teacher is reading, by responding to questioning. They should also be encouraged to take responsibility for spotting cohesion relations in the text, indicating the nature of the problem (if one exists), and indicating or initiating possible inferences. The teacher, at this point, should no longer take primary responsibility for the comprehension monitoring or hypothesis development. Instead, the teacher should direct the students' own efforts by pointing out things they may have missed and reinforcing student efforts.

"It is important to get the dynamic going so that everyone has different ideas as to what may happen. Then reading becomes a game for the students, where they get to see who guessed right" (*1*, p. 26).

In the third and last stage of the technique the students apply the newly learned skills in structured silent reading activities. Students should read passages with specific difficulties to find out what is wrong. For cohesion lessons, the teacher can insert questions periodically to require inferential integration. The following rewritten version of part of the earlier passage conforms to these guidelines.

> The jacket was tight. The zipper slipped down. (Why did the zipper slip?) Out came the nails, right in front of the owner. He was arrested for stealing. (Who was arrested?) John's father was very angry when they called him. (Why was John's father angry? Was it because John had been arrested, or for some other reason?)

After these three stages, the students should begin independently using comprehension monitoring strategies. The teacher can then encourage transfer to other types of reading in other subjects.

Teacher Questioning

The vast majority of questions teachers ask after reading are literal or factual questions, which students can answer using a phrase or sentence from the text. The following sentences and questions, for instance, reflect the most common type of question asked in the classroom.

(1) Andy went to the store. He intended to buy milk for his mother. On his way home, he fell. The bottle broke and he cried.

(2) Where did Andy go?

One can answer this literal question by recalling the first part of the first sentence and inserting the information required by the question. No inference or integration is required.

Note that the group of simple sentences lacks explicit cohesion. A purpose connective is missing between the first and second sentences and a causal connective is missing between the third and fourth sentences. In addition, the reader must infer that it was the *milk* bottle that broke. Questions which reinforce comprehension strategies to overcome these textual limitations are very different from the typical literal recall questions. The following questions, for instance, direct the readers' attention to the missing elements and encourage the use of comprehension strategies.

(3) Why did Andy go to the store?

(4) Where did Andy buy the milk?

(5) What broke? Did anything spill out?

(6) What happened when Andy fell?

These four questions are still close to what most practitioners would call literal comprehension questions, but they actually require an integration of the text information that is not explicitly stated. Thus, answering these questions requires the reader to use background information in making inferences. Additional questions of interest for this small group of sentences include:

(7) Did Andy actually buy the milk? How do we know?

(8) Who cried? Why?

(9) What do you think will happen when Andy gets home?

(10) How do you think Andy feels about breaking the milk bottle?

Notice that the sentences in number 1 do not indicate that Andy actually bought the milk, only that he intended to do so and that there is some relationship between him, milk, and the breaking of the bottle. Question 8 is an anaphora question, since the reader needs to link the pronoun "he" with Andy. The second part of the question and questions 9 and 10 all rely heavily upon the reader's background knowledge, but are not irrelevant, since understanding these issues is crucial for complete understanding of the sentences. The second part of question 8 and question 7 are connective cohesion questions in that the information required for their answer could have been explicitly stated with connectives.

Questions like these which require cohesion inferences and encourage integration with background knowledge should be asked instead of, or at least in addition to, the more common literal recall questions. These questions are not more difficult to ask or to evaluate, although they do require more precise and creative thought on the part of the teacher or the designer of instructional materials. The derivation of this type of question depends upon the recognition of the cohesion relationships in the text. Once areas of text which may present difficulties due to a lack of cohesion are identified, the specific questions needed to address the problem become obvious. It is, of course, the intent of this book to help teachers become aware of these issues and to become adept at recognizing and remediating the problems that ambiguous cohesion relations can cause.

Previewing and Discussing

Previewing is a student centered strategy rather than a teacher centered technique. It is a prereading process which the student can use independently, without teacher presence. However, students need to learn this technique with the guidance of a teacher, as it is rarely spontaneously developed or used. In previewing, the goal is to skim through the passage before actually reading to discover the main ideas and focus of the passage. The student should then review the information in order to develop predictions and to activate relevant background information. Properly learned, previewing can specifically facilitate comprehension of noncohesive text by giving the reader an overview of the text. This overview can provide much of the information needed to deal with any noncohesive elements. Hypotheses about the meaning, intent, structure, and content of the text can be made before reading, making comprehension and inferencing during reading easier. This head start and the possible additional processing capacity it may free during reading should prevent some of the normal comprehension failures caused by noncohesive text.

No hard and fast rules govern the process of previewing. Some individuals prefer to read the first and last paragraphs of a selection quickly, some read the first sentence in every paragraph, some look for italics and boldface (marked text), some skim a few words from each paragraph, and some use a combination of these techniques or their own particular adaptation. A few individuals find that the best overview comes from skimming a passage from the end toward the beginning. Obviously, the method depends not only upon the individual, but also upon the text itself. Content area texts are often best previewed by concentrating on the introduction, concluding summary, section headings, and marked text. Well-written content texts often have a predictable placement pattern for topic sentences, usually in the beginning of paragraphs, which makes paragraph previewing fairly simple. With narrative text, previewing of phrases and sentences on a random basis is usually effective as long as the topic and structure are familiar.

To teach previewing, the first step is to explain its purpose. When students understand why previewing can be functional, they see it as goal oriented and are more likely to be receptive to using it. It is often helpful to point out that though previewing may take a little time, it will usually save time during actual reading, improve comprehension and retention, and therefore improve performance, all with little additional effort. Initial introduction and practice should be on fairly short passages well within the students' independent reading level. Passages that are too difficult will discourage the students. SRA kits often contain material which is both short and at a variety of reading levels allowing a gradual progression from very easy to reading-level-appropriate materials throughout the process of learning to preview.

To insure that the students will not try to "read" the passage during previewing, you might want to start with a time limit. About 60 seconds for average fourth grade readers with appropriately leveled SRA lab cards is reasonable at the beginning, though the time should be cut once they are familiar with the process. More proficient readers may be able to start with less time. Keep the atmosphere light, and encourage students, gently, to try to make it through the entire selection in the allotted time. Tell them to try different strategies for previewing, such as looking for key phrases or topic sentences.

After each previewing exercise, briefly discuss the students' findings and conclusions, since the goal is to teach each student to conduct such a discussion internally before reading. The discussion should center around three areas: the predicted topic and organization of the passage, the information the student already knows from past experiences which is relevant to understanding the passage, and any portions of the text which appear to present comprehension problems. Questions should, therefore, center around the passage and its content, cohesion problems and their possible solutions, and what students already know about the subject. In addition, discuss how previewing helps solve problems. With persistent practice, the students should become comfortable enough with previewing and the teacher/self-questioning that the process will become automatic and no longer require external direction.

The ReQuest Procedure

One of the most exciting comprehension instruction techniques in use today is the ReQuest method by Manzo (5). This procedure is based on reciprocal questioning, in which the student(s) and teacher take turns asking one another questions. The procedure is suitable for all grades, from kindergarten through college (young classes normally use pictures or orally read passages). Narrative and expository text is equally effective, so the technique may be adapted for any class. Though initially advocated for one-to-one instructional settings, ReQuest is equally effective with small groups and whole classes as well as in many areas of comprehension (including cohesion comprehension), depending upon the intent of the instructor and the type of questions asked.

Before the ReQuest session, you need to prepare a passage or materials. The text preparation is simple, involving decisions on places to break the material apart. Typically, text sections of one to three paragraphs work best. (Manzo recommends starting with sentence length units, though these are too limited except in remedial settings.) Short sections are recommended with young students, and older and more proficient individuals can succeed with longer sections. When possible, try to break the passage into logical units according to the content. Divide the sections either by cutting them apart or by indicating to the students an obvious landmark in the text at which to stop. Pictures usually can be easily separated and distributed one at a time. Textbooks, which obviously cannot be cut, can be used quite easily by asking students to read to the start of the paragraph which begins with a particular word. If you are reading a selection to the students for use with ReQuest, simply read it in sections.

Prepare students for a ReQuest activity by 1) discussing the topic of the passage to enhance interest and to activate prior knowledge of the area and 2) setting an informal atmosphere in which the students feel relaxed and understand their role in the task. It is often helpful to present ReQuest as a game-like activity. Many teachers have had success using ReQuest as a reward activity at the end of the day or week.

The basic procedure for ReQuest is to have the entire group, including the teacher, read one short section of a text silently (variations are recommended for specific applications). Then the teacher and student(s) take turns asking each other questions. Usually, the teacher will turn the text over and the students will ask questions. Next, the students turn their texts over and the teacher asks them questions.

Though not defined by Manzo, the most productive aspects of the teacher's role are 1) to reinforce thoughtful questions from the students, particularly those questions which require inferences or which involve cohesion features; 2) to reinforce thoughtful answers and the reasoning behind them; 3) to model appropriate strategies for question-answering techniques, including compensation for noncohesion factors; 4) to model appropriate questioning by asking only inference, prediction, integration, and general cohesion related questions; and 5) to prevent the atmosphere from becoming evaluative by not keeping grades or records, by not responding to either questions or answers in any fashion that could be perceived as negative, and by not getting every student question correct.

For cohesive inferencing, a teacher could concentrate on questions such as, "What makes us believe that (character's name) did (specific action from the text)?" or, "Why did (specific event from the text) occur and what evidence do we have?" Using the brief text about John, Sam, and the nails, the teacher could ask questions like the following:

> Who stole the nails?
> What information in the text makes you think that he was the one who did it?
> Why was John's father angry?
> What other reasons could there be for John's father to be angry?
> Who called John's father?

If students ask the teacher, "Who called John's father?" the appropriate answer might be something like the following:

> The story doesn't really tell us who called John's father, just that "they" called him. The only people in the story who could have called him are John, Sam, or the police. Usually, when a person is arrested, the police allow him or her to make a phone call. Also, when a person who lives at home with parents is arrested, the police usually call the parents. But if John wasn't arrested, his father wouldn't have been called. I think we need more information before we know who called John's father but right now, the most logical answer is that it was John himself, either from the store or from the police station.

This type of modeling by the teacher during ReQuest exercises will help students learn to draw inferences, make predictions, and integrate text. If the teacher emphasizes these skills in questioning, in modeling, and in the reinforcement of both questions and answers, then the student is likely to learn these skills. The advantage of the ReQuest technique is that it provides an effective structure for appropriately teaching cohesion inferencing which includes actual guidance in skill implementation.

The Guided Reading Procedure

Also by Manzo (*4*), the Guided Reading Procedure (GRP) can be used to improve students' reading comprehension and to help train students to deal successfully with noncohesive text. Like ReQuest, it is suitable for most grade levels, subject areas, and classroom formats. GRP is based upon a structure which focuses students on the content of a text and elicits recall. It is probably most successful from the middle grades to the college level and with both small and large groups. Both narrative and expository prose may be used with the technique. The basic procedure is to prepare students for the reading, have them silently read the passage, ask for free recall from the passage, record the recall on a chalkboard, review the selection for missed information, organize or otherwise use the information on the board for comprehension reinforcement and instruction, and discuss the passage.

1. Prepare the students for reading by discussing both the GRP and its goals and the passage itself. Particularly emphasize relating the content of the passage to information with which the students are already familiar.

2. Read and recall the information in the passage. Silent reading is preferable, and the teacher should also act as a role model by reading the passage. Once everyone has read the passage, encourage the students to recall as much information from the passage as possible. As students volunteer the information write it on the board for all students to see. Don't evaluate responses at this time, since the single goal is to maximize recall.

3. Review the text to clarify points already recorded and to add omitted information. At this point, encourage students to go back over the text.

4. Manipulate the information recalled by eliminating duplicate recordings and either sequencing the information (excellent for sequencing skills) or grouping it by topic or category (such as cause and effect — ideal for indicating cohesive inferences). Do this as a group with discussion and debate centering around the reasons for the organization.

5. Take the students beyond the text by discussing the various connections and inferences which are needed to understand the text. Discuss specific entries on the board: how the information items are linked, both explicitly and implicitly, and how the overall structure coordinates all of the information. Focus on the reasoning strategies behind these connections and inferences, clearly indicating how to integrate information with prior knowledge to infer cohesive ties. Any recalled information which was actually an inference (i.e., information which came from the students as part of their contribution to the nature of the text) should be clearly indicated, and any additional inferences made during the discussion should be included on the board.

The GRP can facilitate integration, inferencing, and comprehension of noncohesive text in a number of ways. The recall and review of the text (with the initial recall in clear sight) promote a well educated review of the

material. Such a review will stimulate integration and understanding. The process of organizing and discussing the information on the board provides an opportunity for learning through modeling and will encourage the reasoning processes necessary for the development of the skills needed for understanding cohesion relations. Additionally, students will begin to understand the importance of being able to recall, organize, and infer.

Summary

The typical lack of direct comprehension instruction (*2, 3*) is particularly serious when students are forced to read difficult materials. Noncohesive text, in particular, requires a set of inference skills which are not normally taught in the schools today. The techniques described in this chapter are designed to help in the teaching of those higher-level skills which are so necessary for the successful independent reading of difficult textual material. These techniques can be used to help students read noncohesive text as well as to develop their general comprehension abilities. Moreover, the most common comprehension instructional technique, teacher questioning, can also be successful in helping students learn to comprehend noncohesive text if the questions asked are properly directed at the inferring of cohesive relations.

References

1. Collins, A., and E.E. Smith. *Teaching the Process of Reading Comprehension* (Tech. Rep. No. 182). Urbana, IL: Center for the Study of Reading, University of Illinois, 1980.
2. Durkin, D. "Reading Comprehension Instruction in Five Basal Reader Series," *Reading Research Quarterly,* 1981, *16,* 515-544.
3. Durkin, D. "What Classroom Observations Reveal about Reading Comprehension Instruction," *Reading Research Quarterly,* 1978-1979, *14,* 481-533.
4. Manzo, A.V. "Guided Reading Procedure," *Journal of Reading,* 1975, *18,* 287-291.
5. Manzo, A.V. "Improving Reading Comprehension through Reciprocal Questioning," unpublished doctoral dissertation, Syracuse University, 1968.